Gergely Papp

1938–1963
Ecsegfalva,
Hungary

COLLECTED BY
Tibor Miltényi

COMPILED BY
The Archive of Modern Conflict

WORDS BY
David Franklin
Tibor Miltényi

BONE IDLE BOOKS

PUBLISHED BY
Bone Idle
65 Queen St. W
Suite 2400, Toronto
ON M5H 2M8
Canada

EDITORS
Parker Kay
Thomas Szlukovenyi

DESIGNER
Julia Troubetskaia

TRANSLATOR
Mark Baczoni

COPY EDITORS
Jess Carroll
Oliver Fugler

PROOFREADER
Julia Salisbury

PRINTED BY
SYL L'art Gráfic Premium
Barcelona, Spain

DISTRIBUTED IN THE UK
AND EUROPE BY
Antenne Books Limited
Studio 55
Hackney Downs Studios
17 Amhurst Terrace
London E8 2BT
United Kingdom
+44 (0) 203 582 8257
antennebooks.com

DISTRIBUTED IN NORTH
AND SOUTH AMERICA BY
D.A.P. Distributed
Art Publishers, Inc.
75 Broad St.
Suite 630, New York
NY 10013
+1 (0) 212 627 1999
artbook.com

WITH SPECIAL
THANKS TO
Glen Brent
James Welch
Kalev Erickson
Luce Lebart
Michael Smith
Michelle Wilson
Stefanie Petrilli

Gergely Papp

Introduction

Written by
David Franklin

Born in 1922, provincial Hungarian photographer Gergely Papp's first photographs date from around 1938, his practice ending abruptly in the early 1960s. Papp was an entirely pragmatic operator of the camera in a way that a professional with artistic aspirations would have evolved away from; the photographs he took are unusual and without easy parallel despite his humble origins. Although he clearly had strong and occasionally antagonistic attitudes towards life and society, Papp was not a dissident photographer because he was not consciously political, with one late but significant exception. As an outsider on nearly every level—physical, social and intellectual—he achieved nothing lasting with his art, and had nothing to express, beyond commemorating his surroundings. However, there is a defiance in that casual viewpoint that makes him all the more compelling today. The most complete treatment of the photographer to date, the goal of this book is to retrieve Papp from isolation and return him to the stream of history by appreciating his small narratives, even if he will stay forever outside the esteemed, progressive tradition of Hungarian photography. If we ignore the margins, however, we understand the centre less well, and he is an exceptional test case for this observation. Papp's photographs brought him some recognition after his discovery by Tibor Miltényi shortly before the photographer's death in 2000. Miltényi is responsible for all of the publications on his work to date, including an essay in this volume, and stands as a singular eyewitness for the artist's words and behaviour.

As a functionally illiterate and dyslexic individual, the camera gave Papp the freedom and objective means to produce finished work in a society that valued labour and physical activity. Whatever Gergely learned about photography would have been from his brother István, who was a part-time photographer, but he seems to have had no awareness of the history of the medium, let alone any contemporary avant-garde. Photography for Papp was an act of defiance that gave him a degree of pride and confident purpose, his path to partial acceptance and control. As a disabled man in a closed, rural society, photography offered a non-verbal means of communication comparable to his beloved clarinet, which he would often play well into the night for locals in the village tavern. With his camera, he created an alternative world in which he could triumph—an escape from his quotidian condition, a new visual world for someone with an uneasy relationship to reality. It was also his only way to please and find temporary acceptance among the locals, and later, his military unit. It must have provided him with joy and no risk or danger to his life (of the kind he faced without the camera because of his physical and mental state and combative personality).

For Papp the camera was primarily for making portraits, giving away the paper prints to the sitters, as entirely private transactions without commercial intent. Yet even if he did not photograph as a full-time pursuit and had no sense of exhibition or a market, he was not truly an amateur in the sense of a dilettante operating for private pleasure. He clearly recognised that he was recording his environment and was rightly proud of that, yet his approach was too unstructured to be classified as documentary. Collectively, what he produced does not constitute a history as he had no overriding agenda, or sense of a structured long-term ambition with his photography. Again, the generally poor condition of the negatives adds further support to this analysis preferring chaos over discipline.

Papp's personal collection of photographs was either dispersed or entirely destroyed when locals, who seem to have had long-standing grievances against him for his anti-social character, ransacked his house right after his death. While his images were never censored, his entire person was deliberately obliterated leading to the ruination of a core body of work with his passing. The cruel goal was to erase him from local knowledge as an act of revenge because of an antagonism to his existence. A fragmentary corpus remains of some 300 images: no traceable originals, a few negatives and later exhibition prints. Thus, one can only generalise about his approach and imagery.

Studying Papp is like studying an ancient Greek sculptor, attempting to appreciate the work second hand with no known originals. A number of previously published images are already missing. The deteriorated condition of many of the negatives caused by their neglect seems appropriate to the spontaneous quality of the photography and the lifestyle of the artist. Papp never ordered or properly stored and archived his own work.

Consequently, we have taken some chronological liberties in arranging the catalogue of
images in this book.

In assessing what survives,
however, Papp did leave us with
a singular testimony of a particularly remote location in Central Europe—his
village of Pusztaecseg (Ecsegfalva) in Eastern Hungary—before, during and after the
war years. Without his camera, the place and
period in which he resided would be virtually
irrecoverable and never seen by outsiders.
Papp glorified the place he lived in the direct
way photography can, and otherwise its
unpretentious people, places and customs
would have been only little remembered. He
presents us with a unique visual record of
these individuals, his neighbours and army
cohorts. Specifically for his village, he printed
the index of a provincial culture only slowly
touched by urbanity or modernity, including
a wide range of human themes and subjects
such as babies, children, school, sport, swimming, hunting, fishing, weddings, pregnancies
and funerals, even a new ditch.

Papp's work can be divided into
three chronological periods: his
time spent in his village just
before the war; his time spent during part of
WW2; and the Communist era, until he sud-
denly ceased to practice in the 1960s. From
a local portraitist, Gergely became something of an adventurer with his conscription
into the Hungarian army late in 1943, which
resulted in his more unusual and ambitious
images as unit photographer, more as a wit-
ness than a combatant. Although the enemy
is never visible he also produced incredibly
poignant images of men under stress, who
could be vulnerable for the camera, often
touching one another lightly on the shoulders
when portrayed in groups. During wartime,
the images he captured can be tenderly
uplifting, as if he provided catharsis to the
awkward fear present in the men's faces and
posture. In some, the deterioration of the
negatives foreshadow the death and disap-
pearance of the sitters. Papp was physically
injured in September 1944 during an ill-fated
training exercise, and eventually taken pris-
oner. The predominantly local lineage of
these photographs becomes especially significant during the later phase of his practice,

as the youthful faces of farmers reappear as
soldiers and eventually Communist citizens.
The abrupt and awkward shift to the Communist period is evident as the photographs
become murkier and more disorganised.
The subjects often seem uncomfortable in
their baggy clothing. This last period produced some of his first consistent still lifes,
absent of people except for the inevitable
images of Stalin. Papp reveals in the bearing
of his neighbours the pressure and out-
rage imposed by history and their profound
attachment to local life. People queue in a
shop in one image oblivious to the incon-
gruous slogan above their heads reminding
them the Fatherland will progress if they
achieve good marks in school. Underlying
humanity and humour is fully apparent: his
imagery never comes across as melancholy
or exploiting any poverty or depravation that
doubtless existed in his village.

Papp was taken seriously as
an official photographer of sorts
judging by the range of his subjects, and was clearly a persuasive person
with camera in hand, able at times to secure
unguarded images: the local bathing beau-
ties, for example. The war pictures especially
suggest a pride and credibility that arose
from his position as company photographer.
With the possible exception of an itinerant
photographer appearing in town, this was the
only time many of these people would have
had their images captured and a moment
of mutual wonder was experienced. During
that period in Eastern Hungary, the taking of
a picture was still a novel experience. Papp
attempted to pose his subjects as best he
could manage judging by the repetitive
arrangements, but the locals also enjoyed
posing themselves and occasionally ham-
ming it up: the taking of the photograph was
a collaborative act with a sense of occasion,
frequently with spontaneous humour. Individuals are often dressed up in their finest
clothing, revealing careful preparation for the
special moment. The photographs capturing
athletics are striking examples of the pop-
ulace enjoying a whole event. People frequently look directly into the lens, transfixed.
The locals were mostly directly involved and
complicit in the image-making, but some
seem bewildered, as if they regretted it after

agreeing to the depiction. Accidentally or not the innocence of children is always well-expressed. Sometimes bystanders look over the shoulder of the man with the camera, or participate in the act of picture taking, as in holding blankets to form a backdrop. Papp introduces or discovers backdrops to keep the subject forward to the camera and close off the potentially distracting distance; leaves, plants, carpets and walls were his favourite devices—a rare indulgence of artifice. He seems to have found his confidence to take his picture when a sitter was seated or had something behind or around them locating them in space. Otherwise, there are few props, with the exception of bouquets of flowers. With such backgrounds and props, one feels Papp believed they should be included but he did not utilise them with much deliberate purpose or decorative intent.

His photographs are not aesthetically distinguished but often memorable because of the place and its imagery, and the unique ways that they were captured. Assuming Papp received some technical instruction from his brother, he nonetheless absorbed no style, but created directly to grasp a personal, more accidental way of looking and perceiving. Working in isolation, he photographed the same way, one imagines, as he played his clarinet, as a persistent amateur with an instinctive fluency grounded in repetition. Papp was disarmingly direct and tender, and highly intuitive. He was not probing of his subjects but revealing with an awkward, always inwardly deflected honesty. The photographs themselves can be characterised by a gentle eloquence and warm tenderness, even if Papp was not seeking any emotion other than wonder, magic and personal esteem. There is no rhetoric, condescension or allegory, no poetry or atmosphere, and yet his personality emerges through the very lack of pretense and the formal limitations, aided by the dependable mechanical action of the camera. He was single-mindedly humble and joyous in his approach, sometimes ambitious in arranging multi-dimensional set pieces that involved seemingly the entire village. A few examples attest to the creation of a broad comedy and staged fiction in cliché, but these are rare. He is mostly very direct and prompt, frequently recording for posterity errors in the arrangement of his scenes.

Because of his lack of technical skill and the way he experienced the world, the spontaneous and accidental are often recorded and give many of his images a unique visual identity. The swimming pool pictures, for example, have a particular unintentional, hypnotic beauty. The representation was worth everything to him, never the artifice, as evidenced through formal mistakes where heads are entirely cut off, eyes are closed, group compositions teeter off balance, people look backwards away from the camera, images are congested with too many subjects, casual bystanders are not cropped out, horizons are tilted, and we see evidence of technical errors like out-of-focus blurring. When Papp casts his own shadow into the image or fails to adjust the lighting well, one assumes he did so accidentally. These were all true accidents and not deliberate artistic statements but nonetheless part now of how we appreciate Papp's work. All of his photographs have the implicit character of ramshackle self-portraiture.

The existence of actual self-portraits throughout his career also implies a pride in the act of photography itself and a self-conscious search for purpose, as well as a degree of personal vanity. He is perfectly dapper in one surviving instance. Despite the pressures to conform socially, the camera offered Papp the freedom to act and even express anti-communist views in one late instance. He is never consciously ideological but in what is thought to be his last picture, with the deliberately felled trees in his own orchard, does suggest the camera could be, for him, a way to exact revenge on an enforcement of Communist society to seize his property—an act of intentional petulance not without personal danger. With knowledge of its context, it is one of his few photographs to take on a truly profound commentary, as opposed to merely recording. Gergely Papp had no legacy; as a creator, he was entirely self-contained and such acts remained private, destined to be futile statements but for our recovery of what could be recovered still. These self-portraits, like all of his photographs, allowed him to stamp time with his camera for a portion of his singular life.

Selected Images

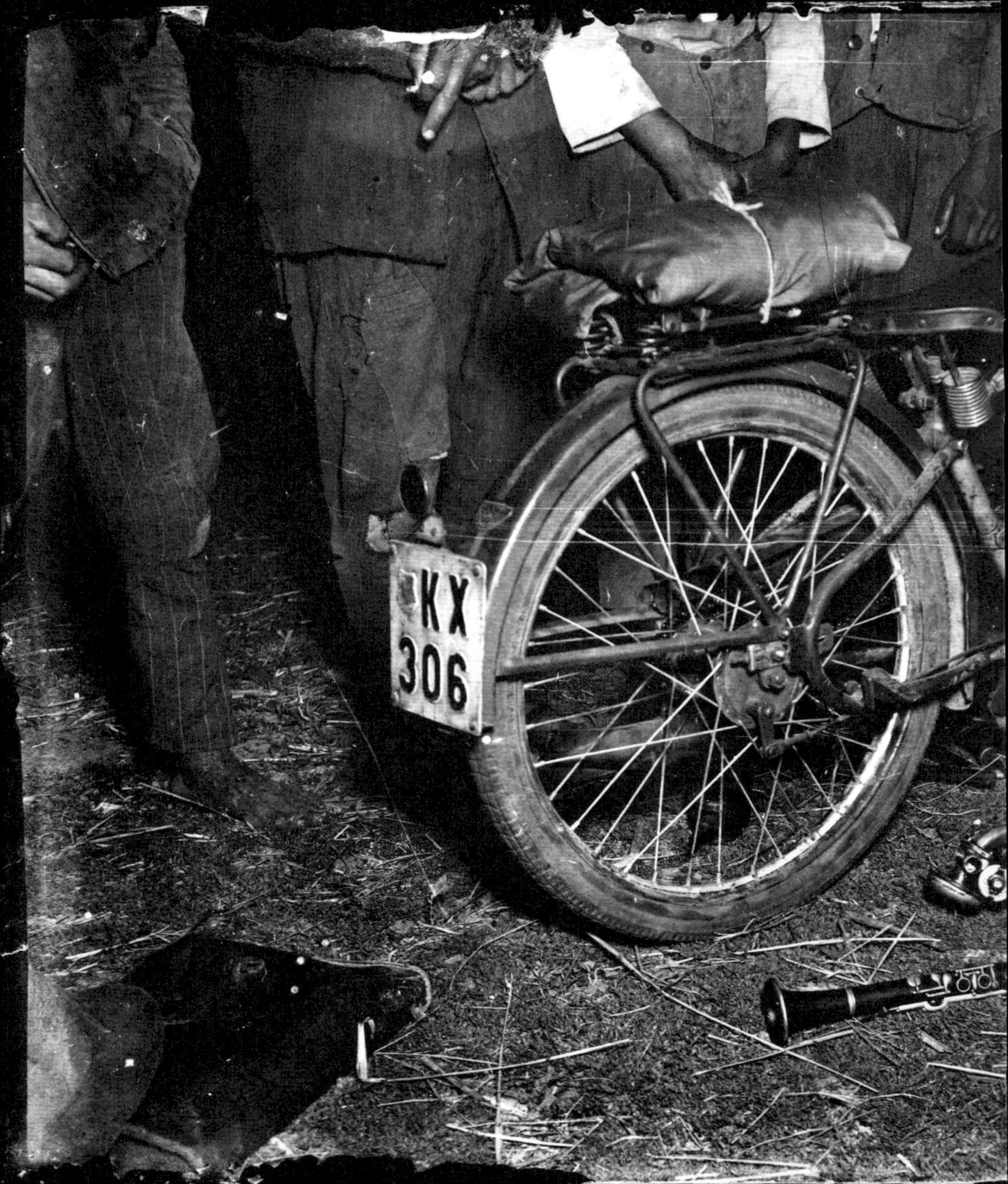
KX
306

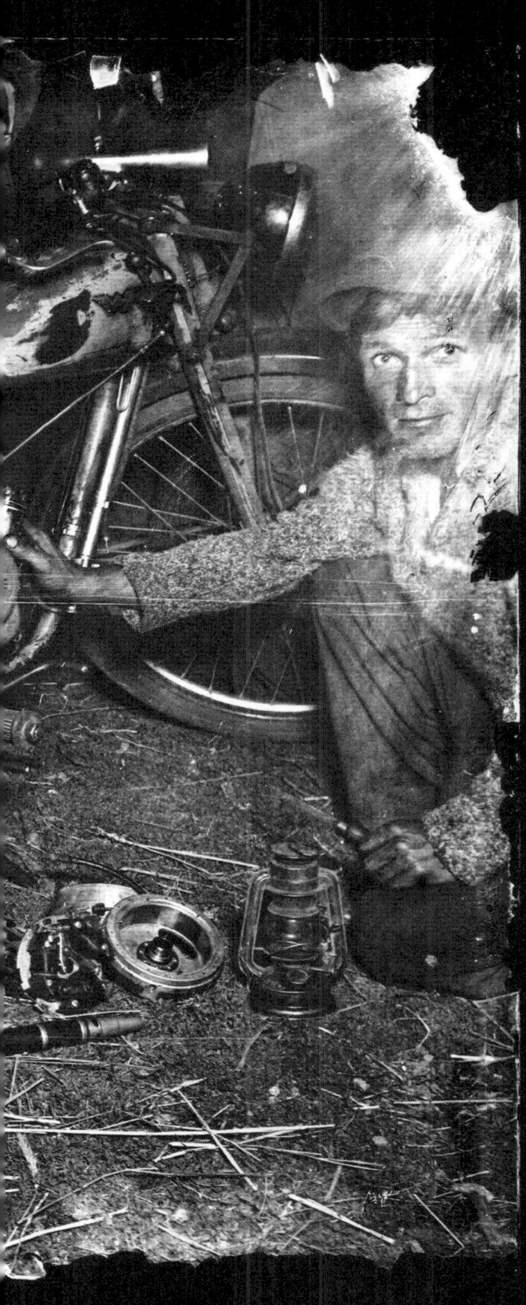

01

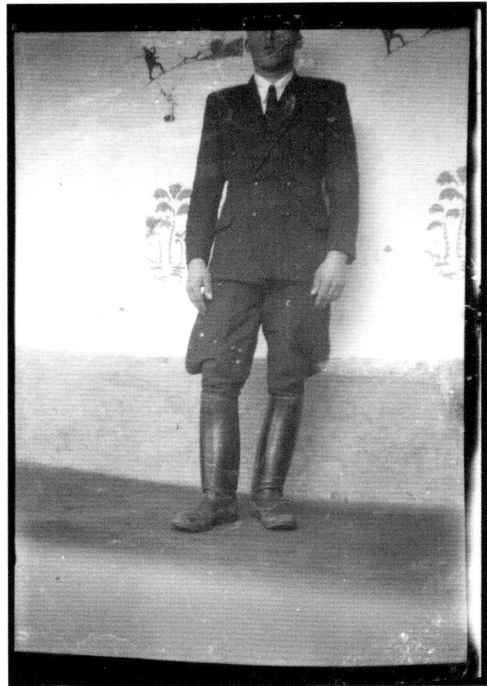

02

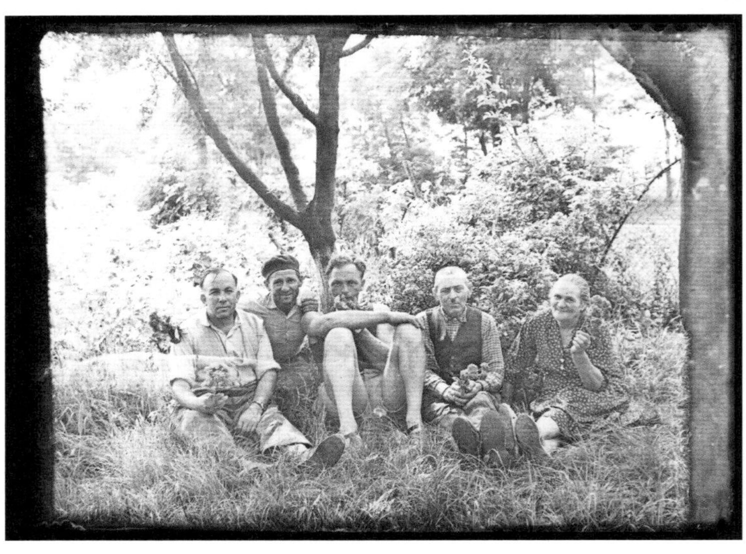

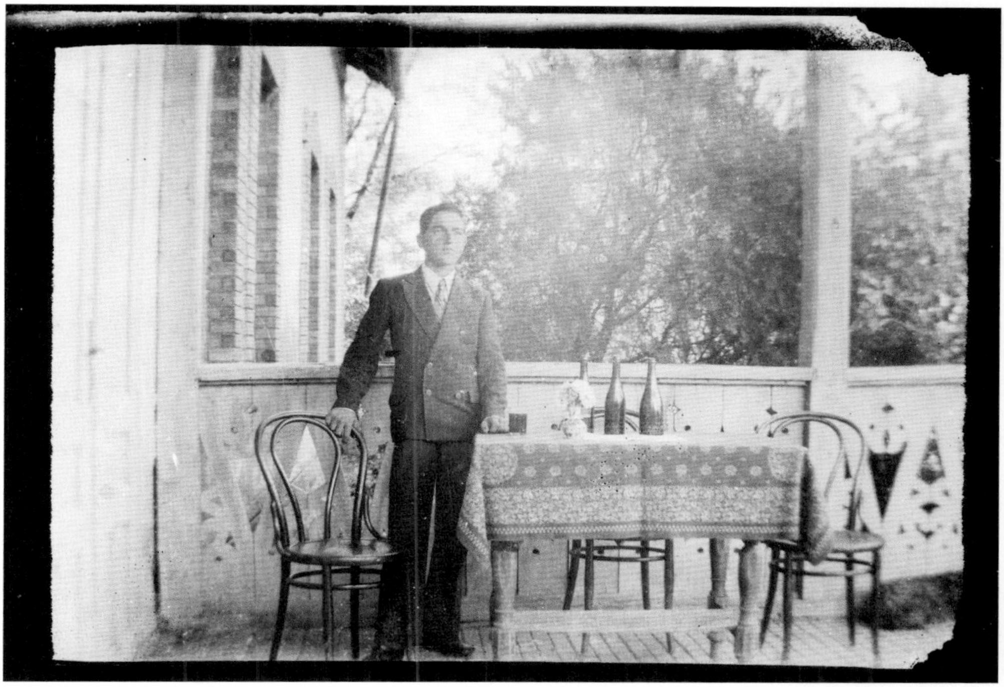

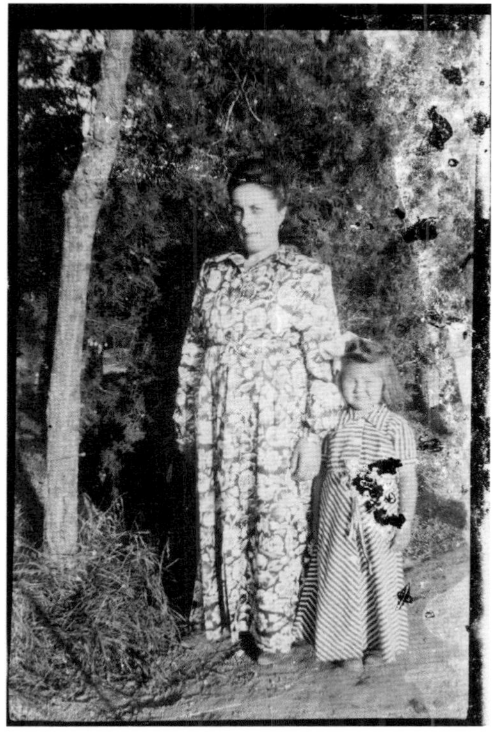

04

05

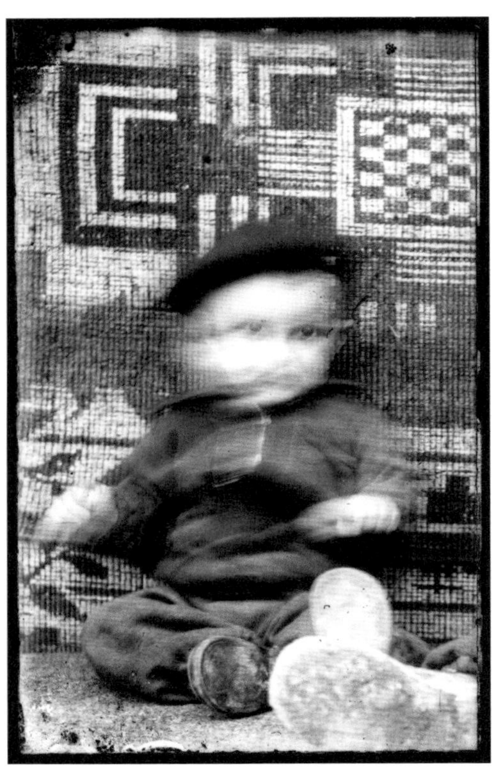

06

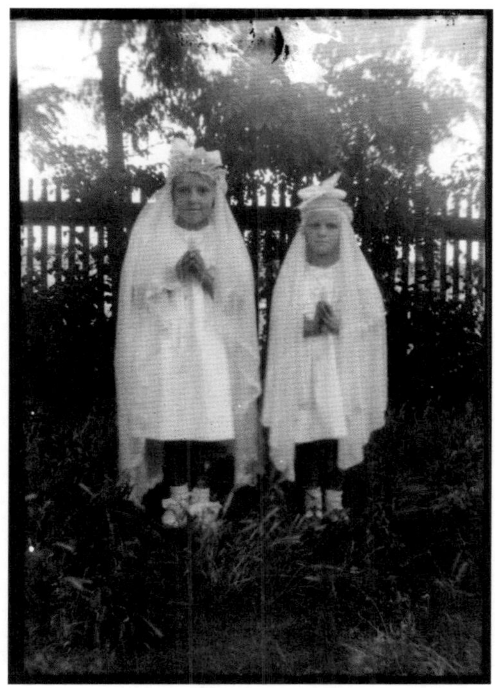

07

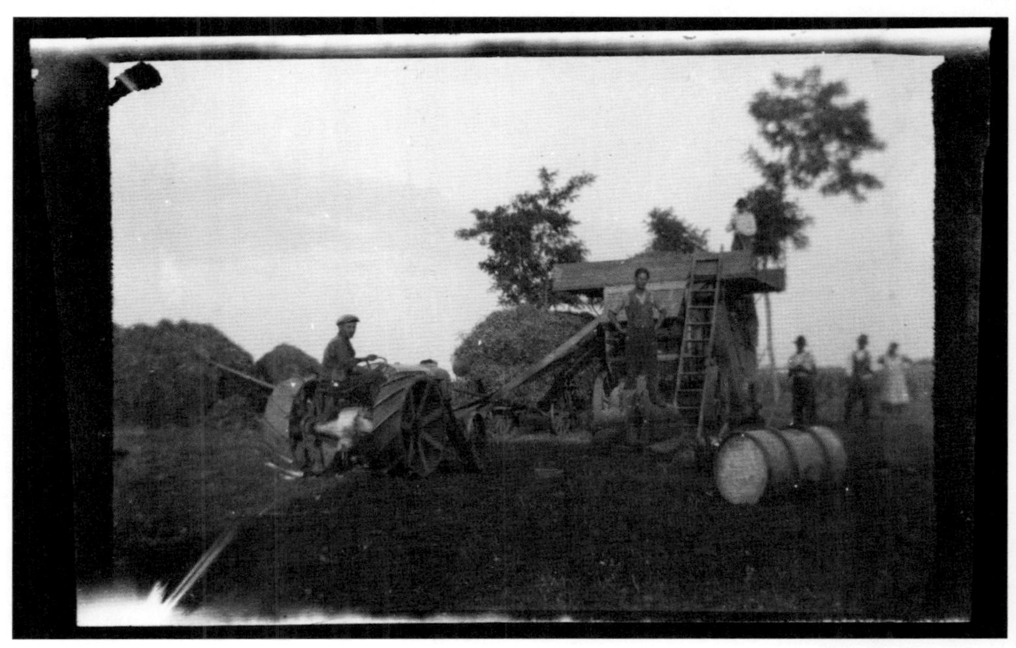

08

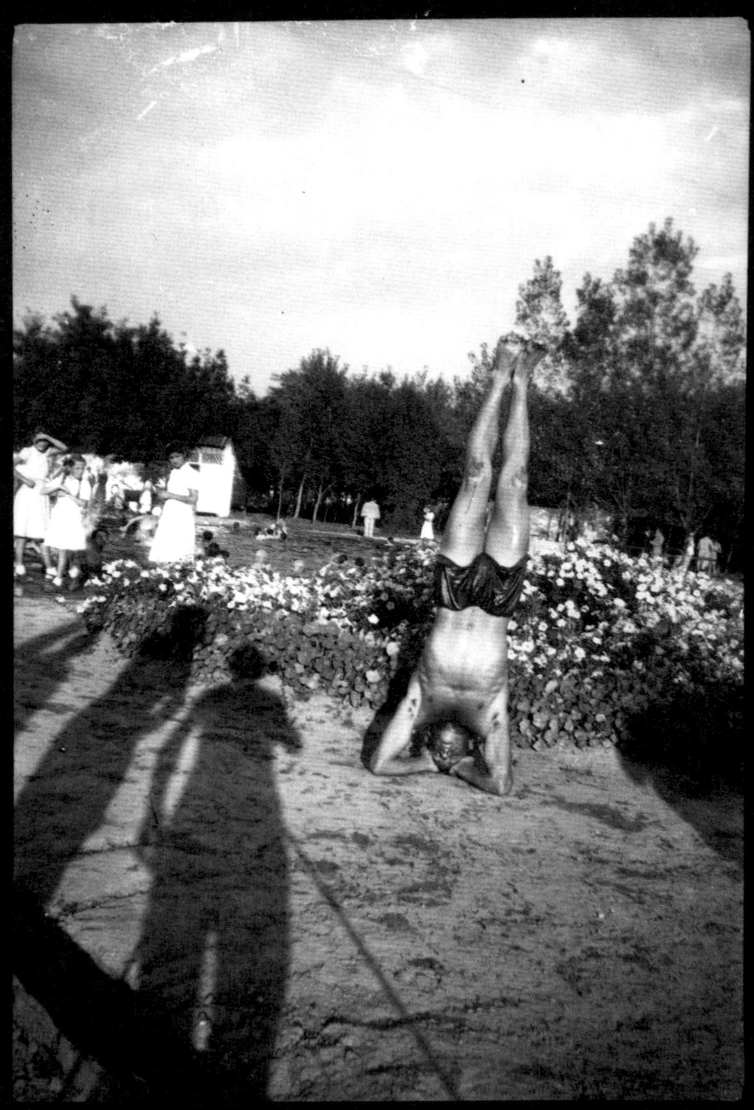

09

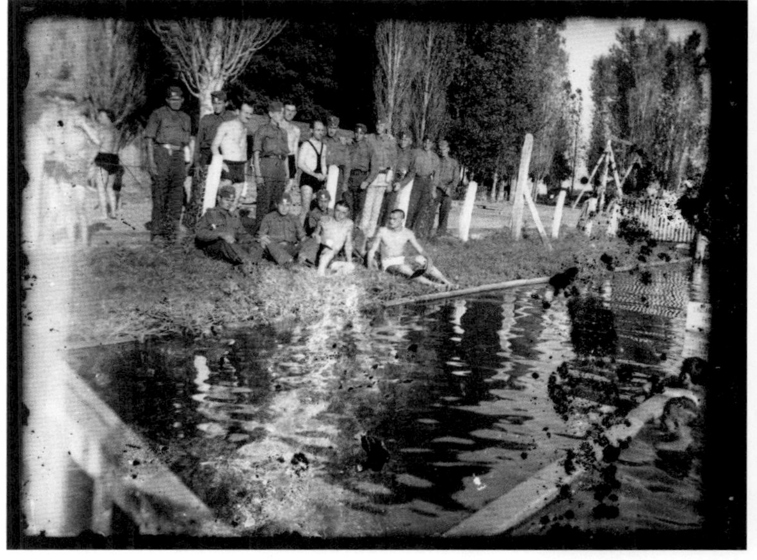

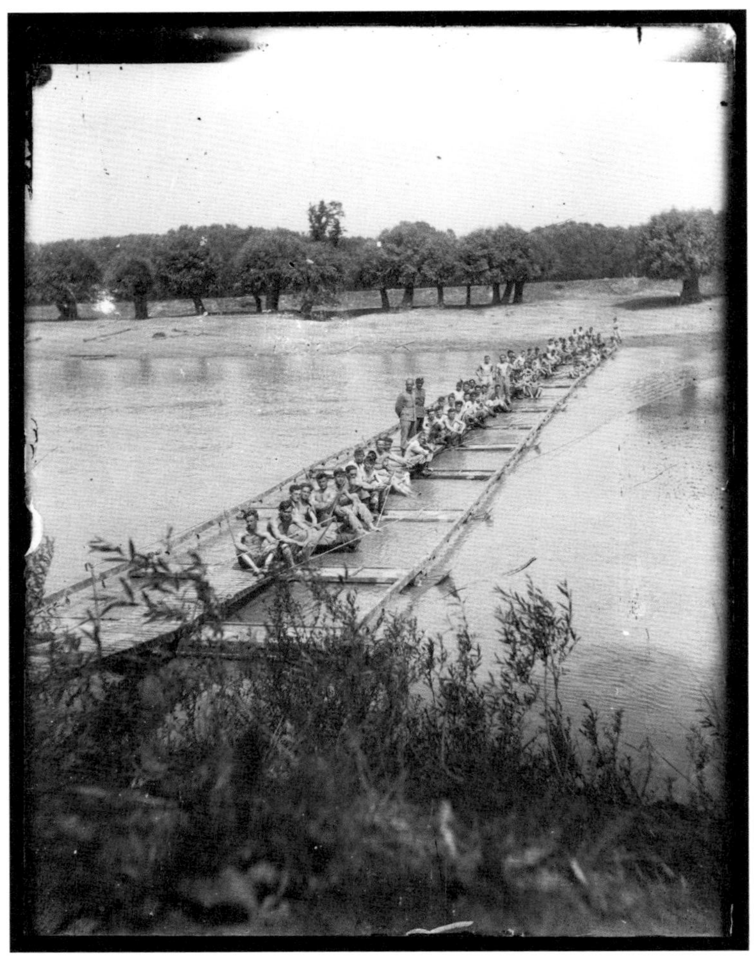

11

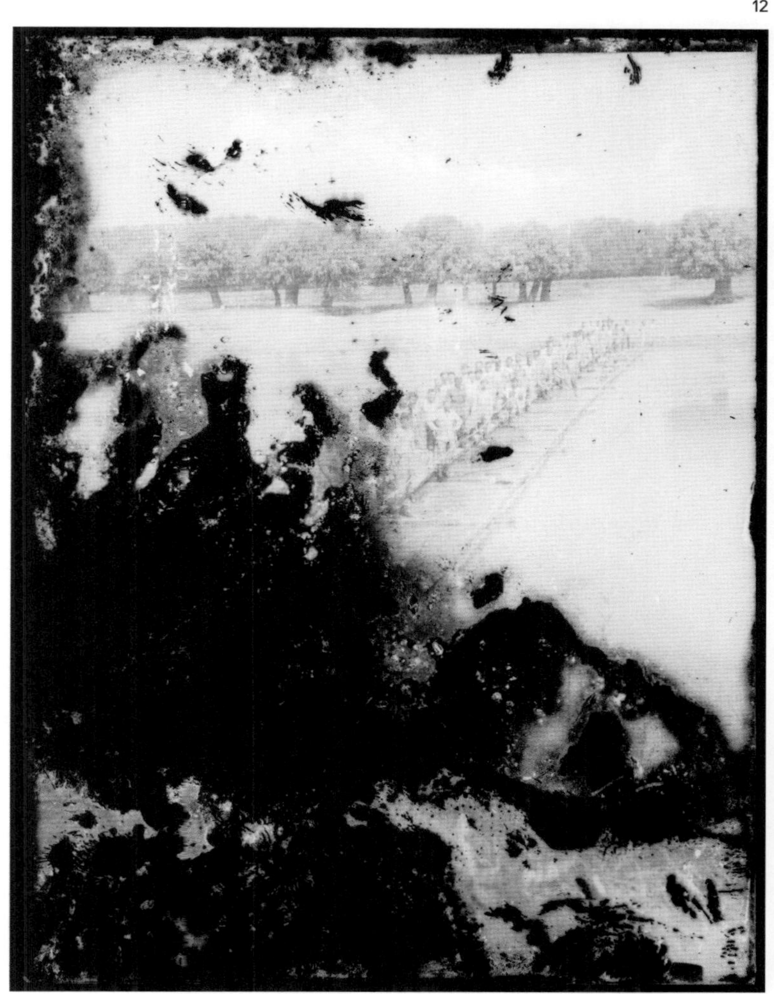

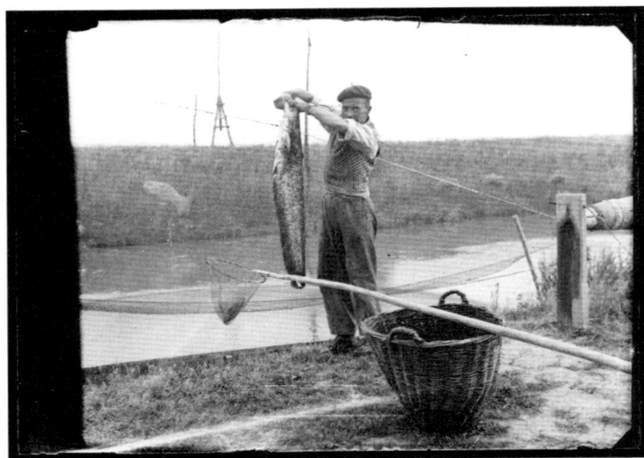

13

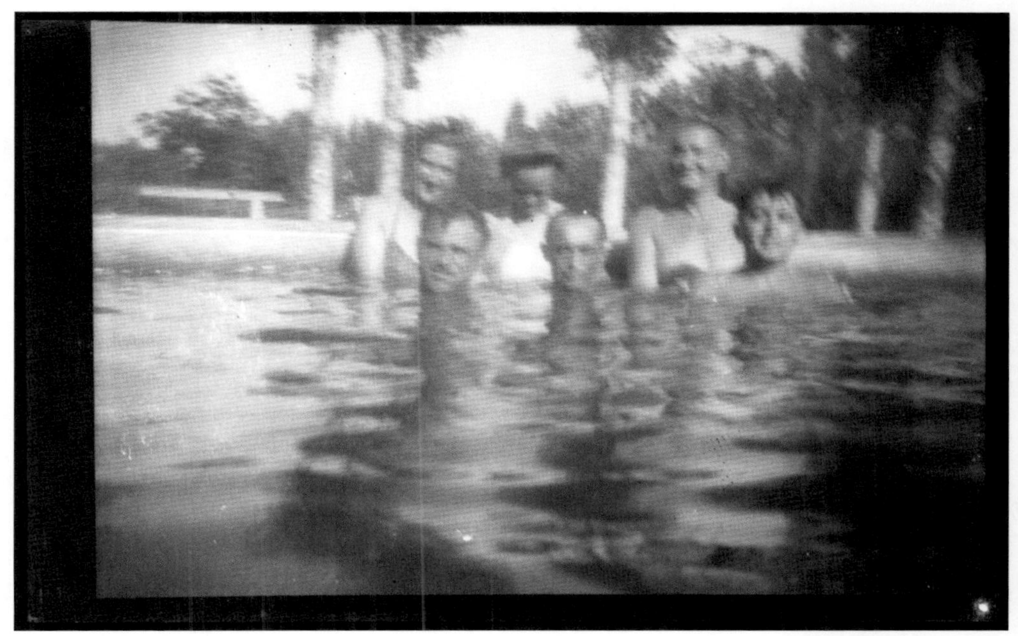

14

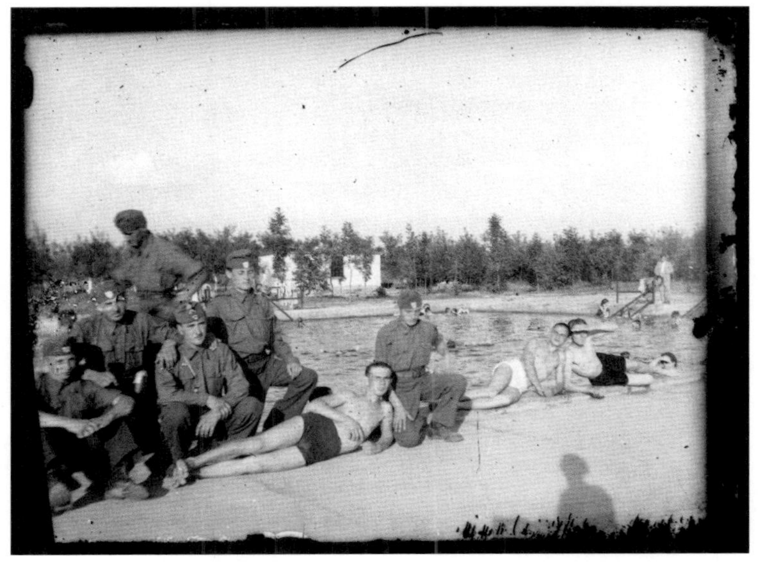

15

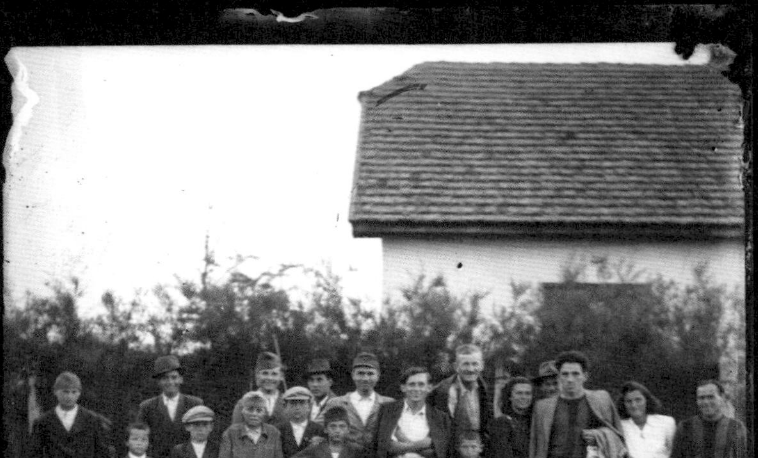

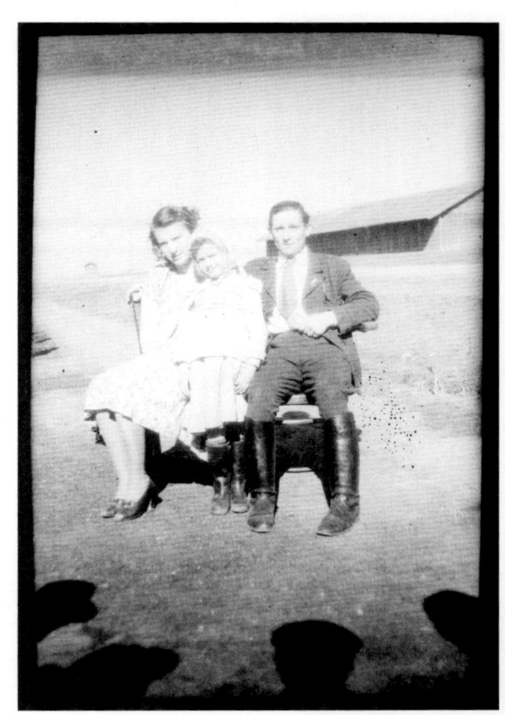

17

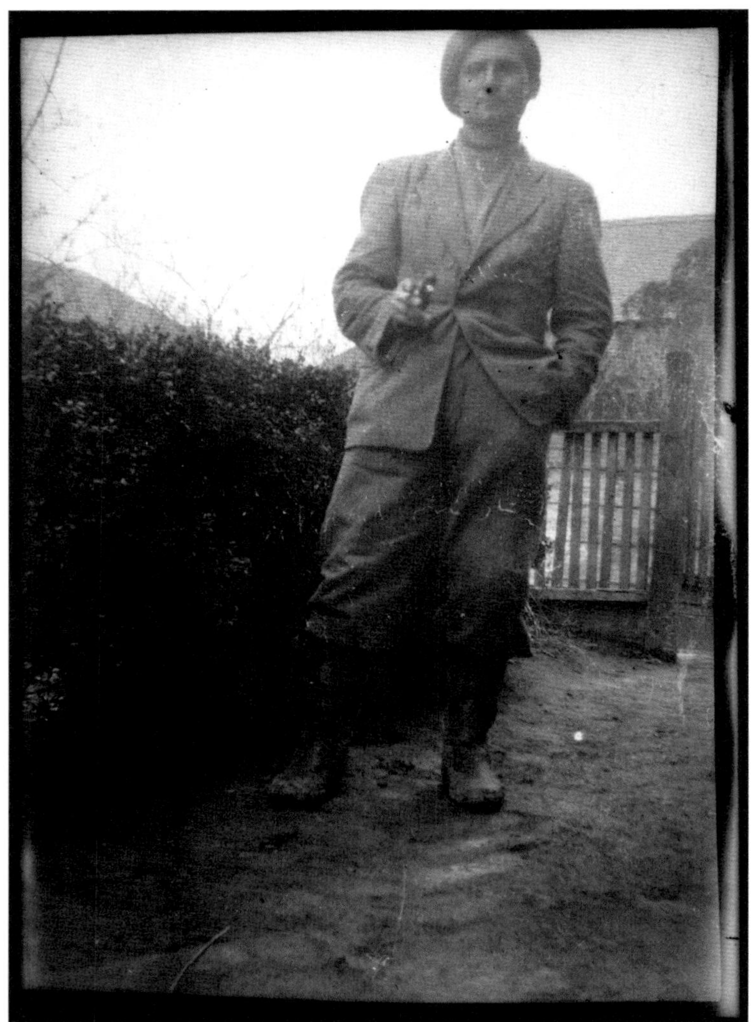

18

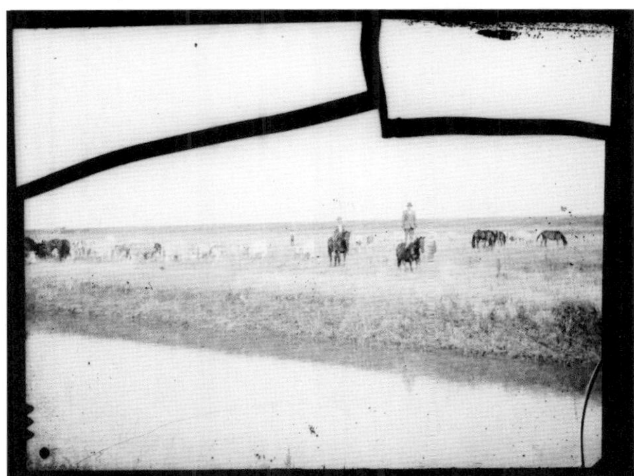

19

20

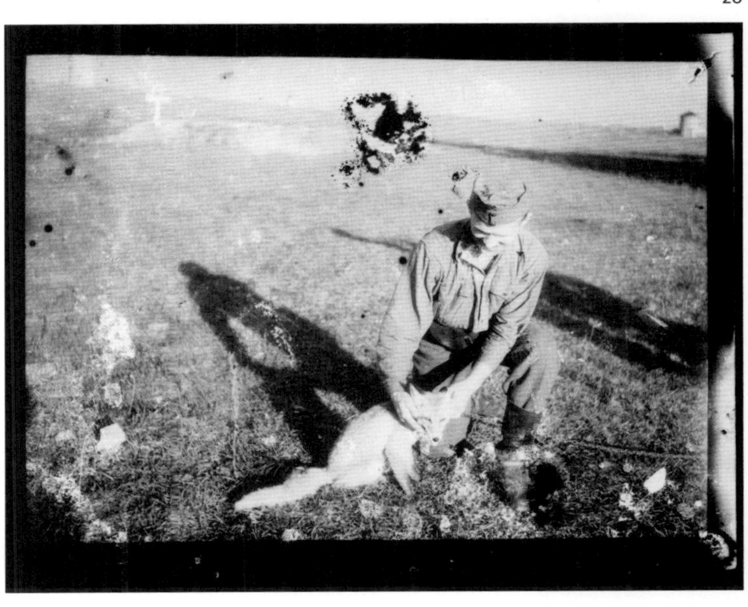

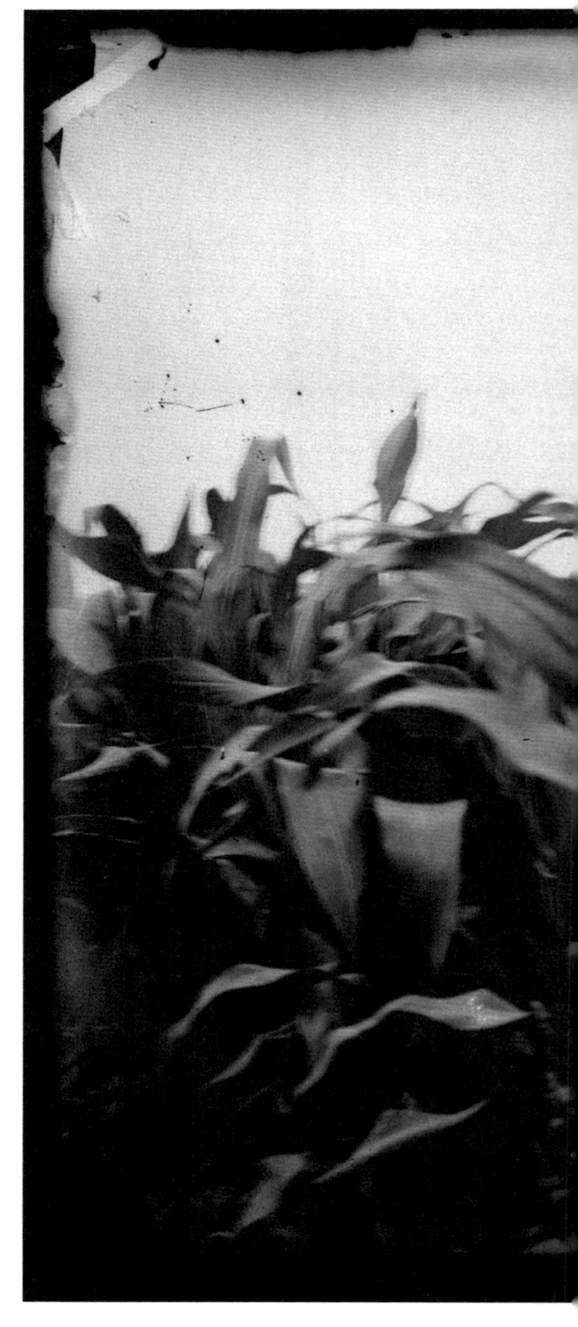

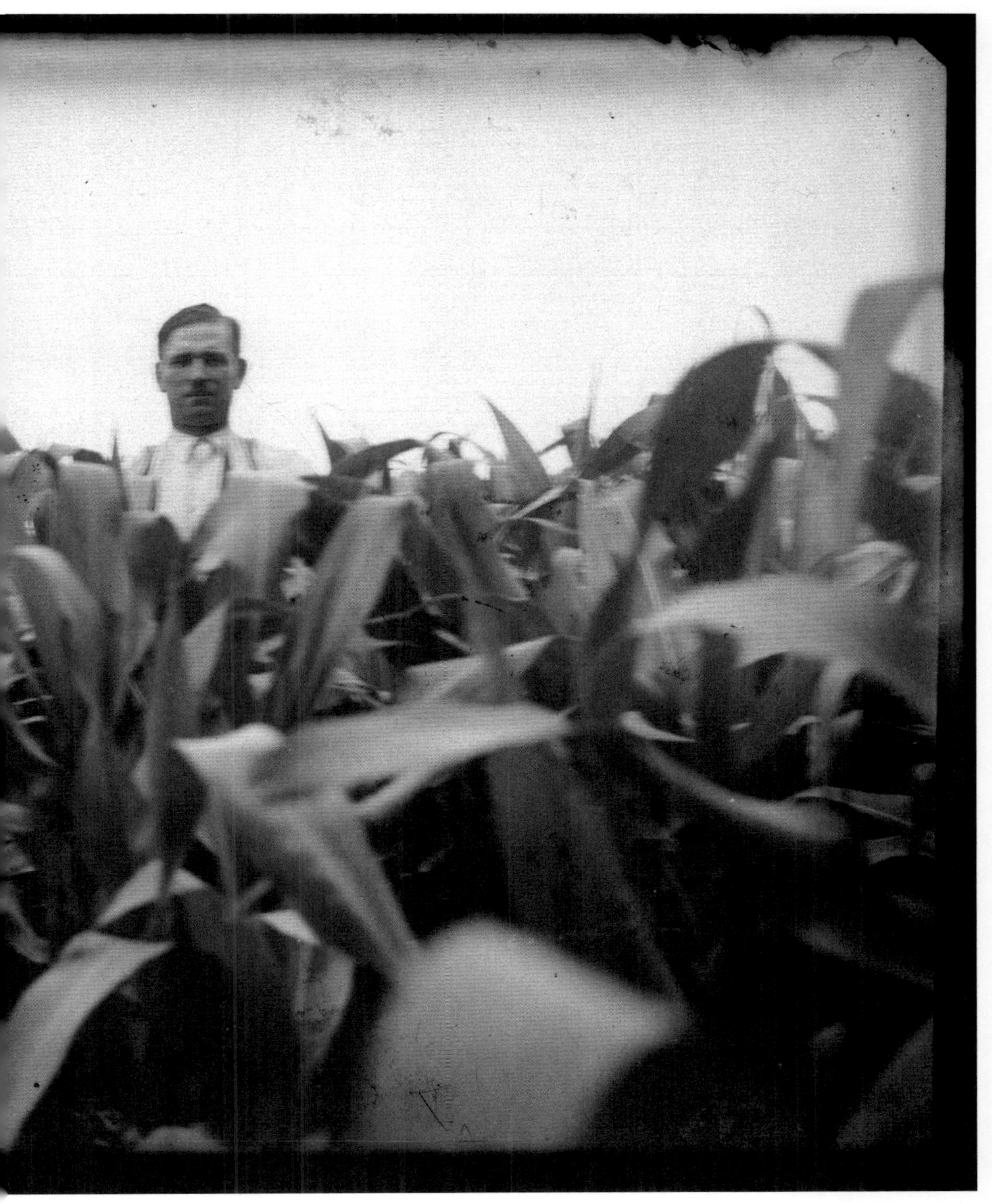

21

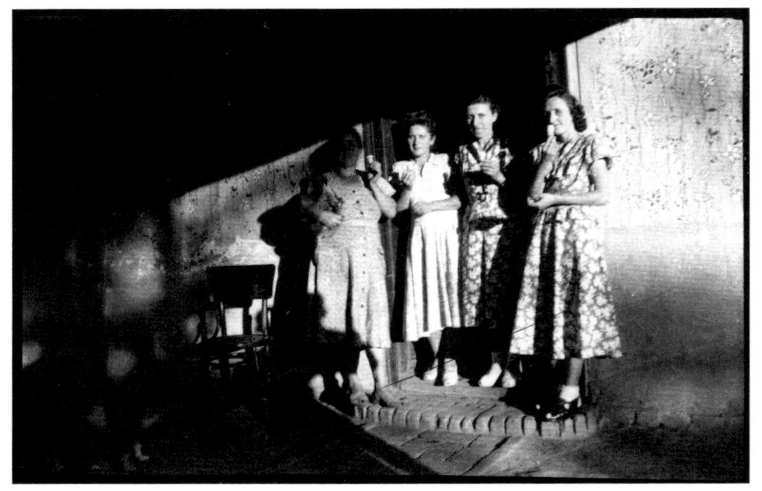

22

23

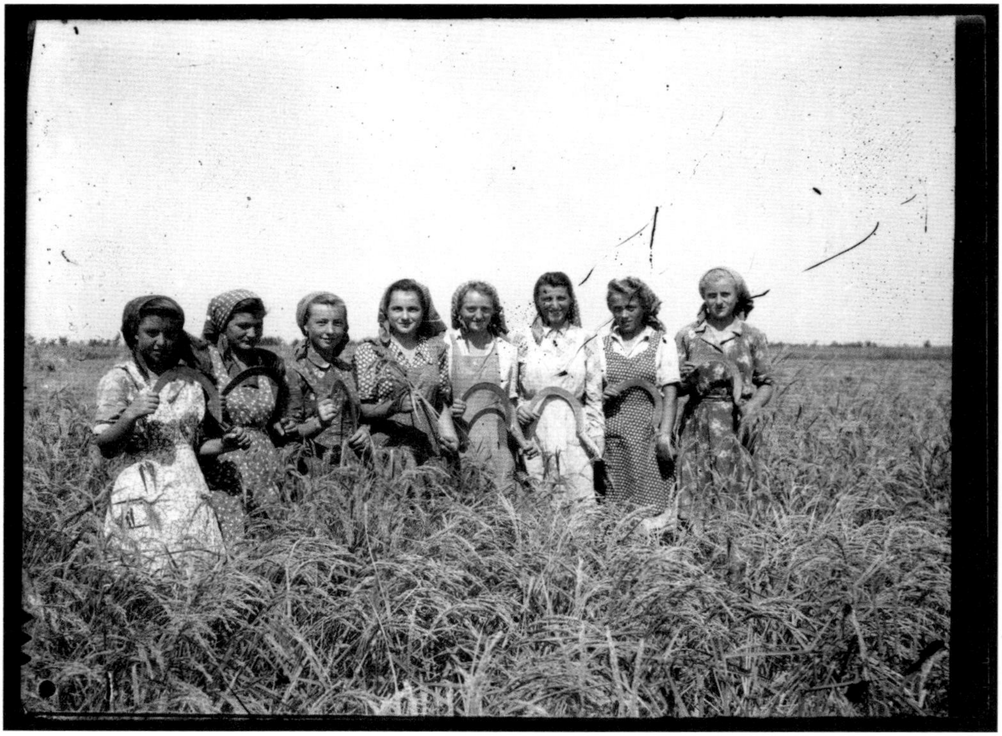

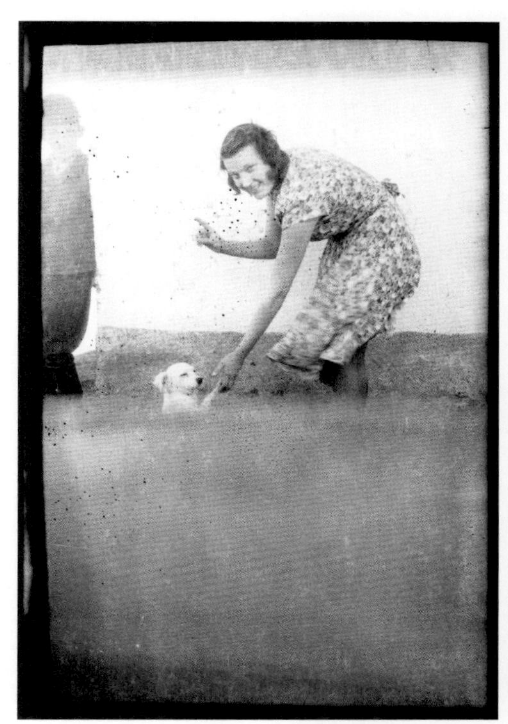

24

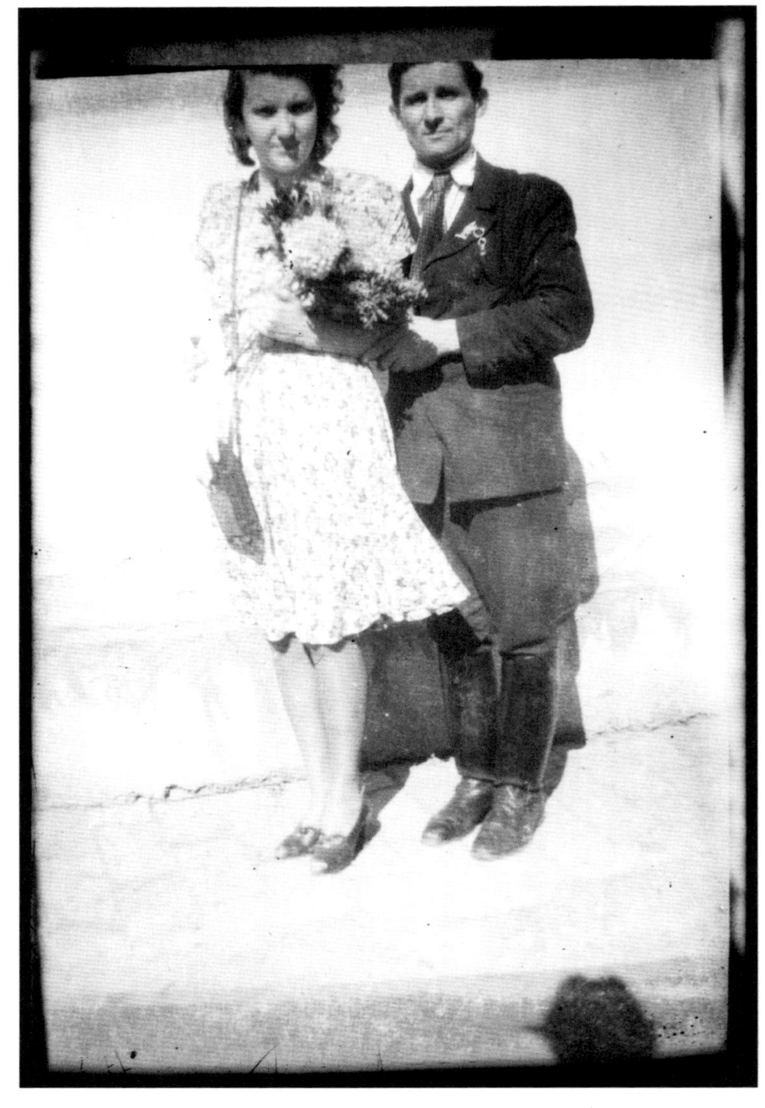

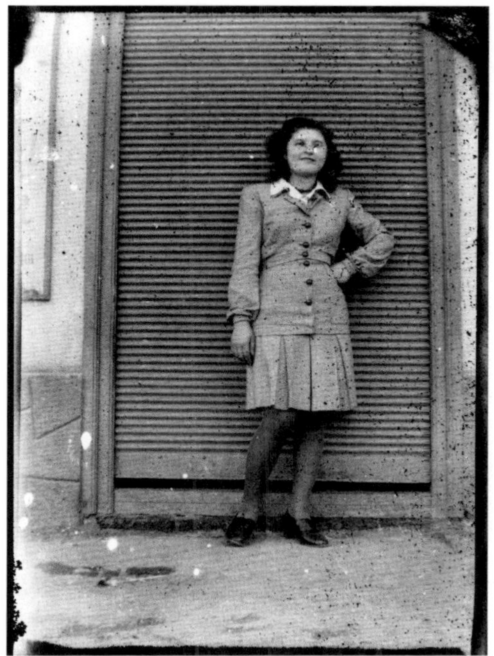

26

27

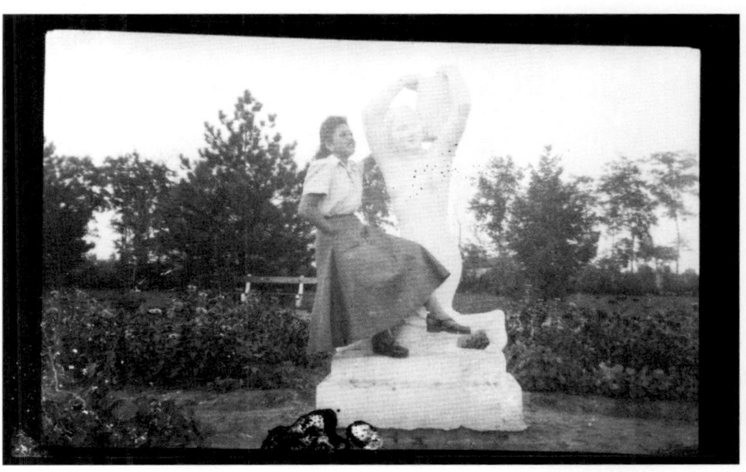

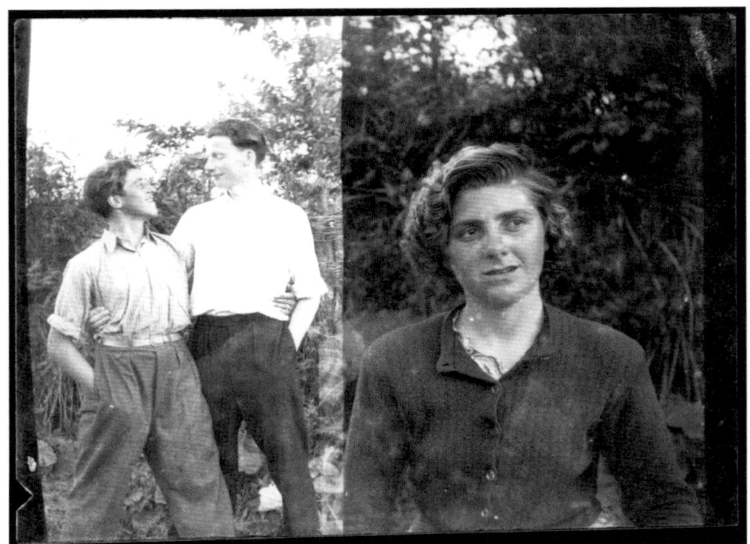

28

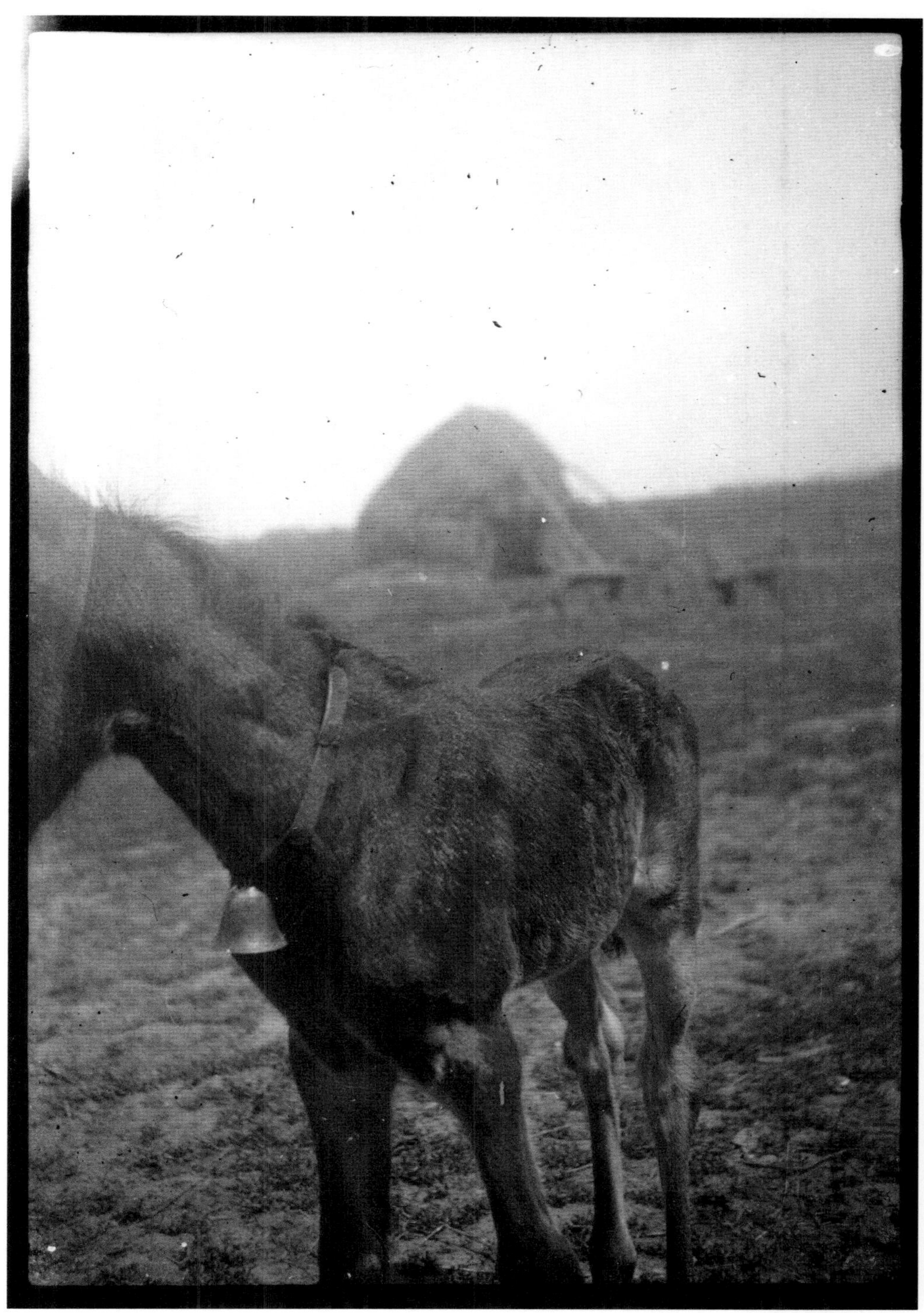

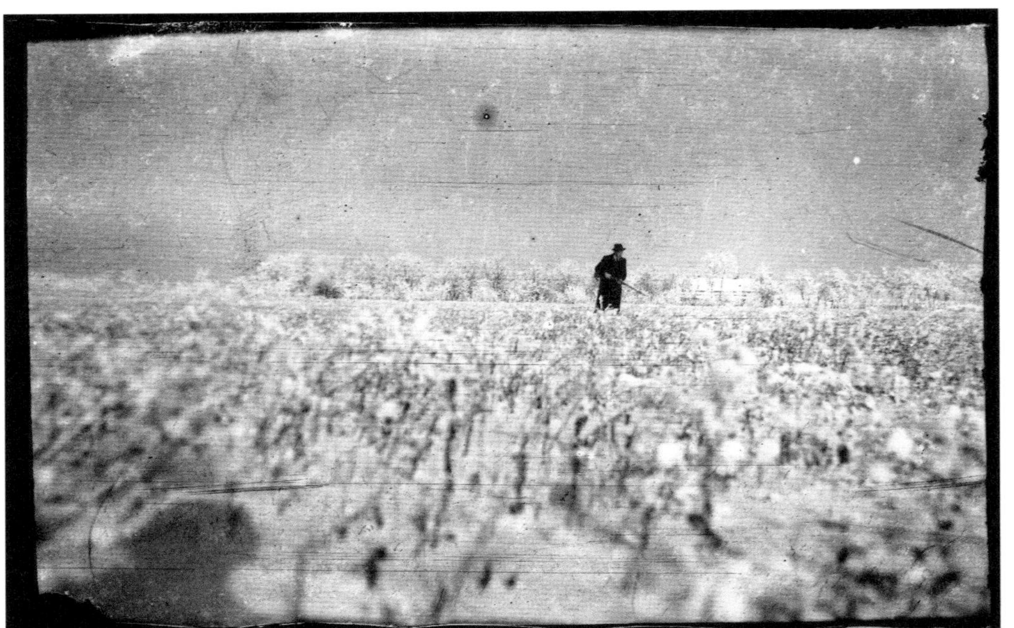

30

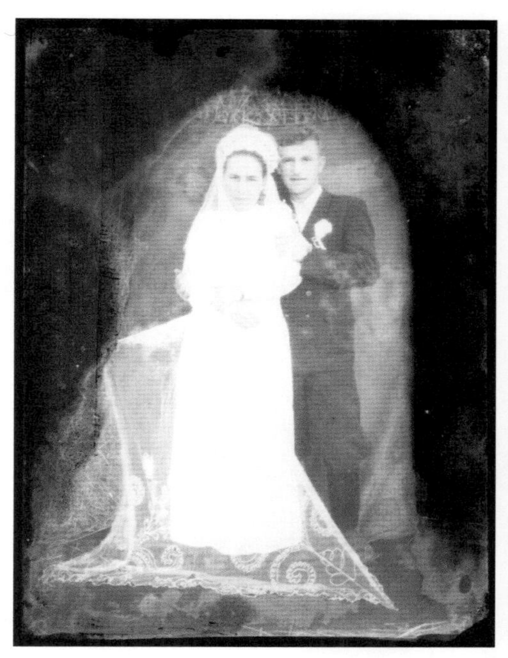

31

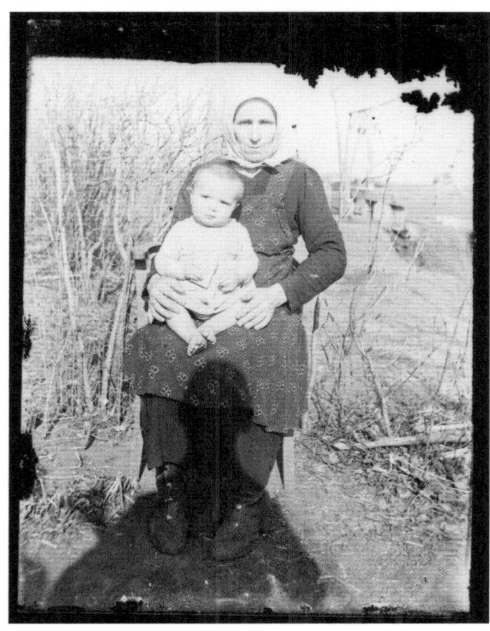

32

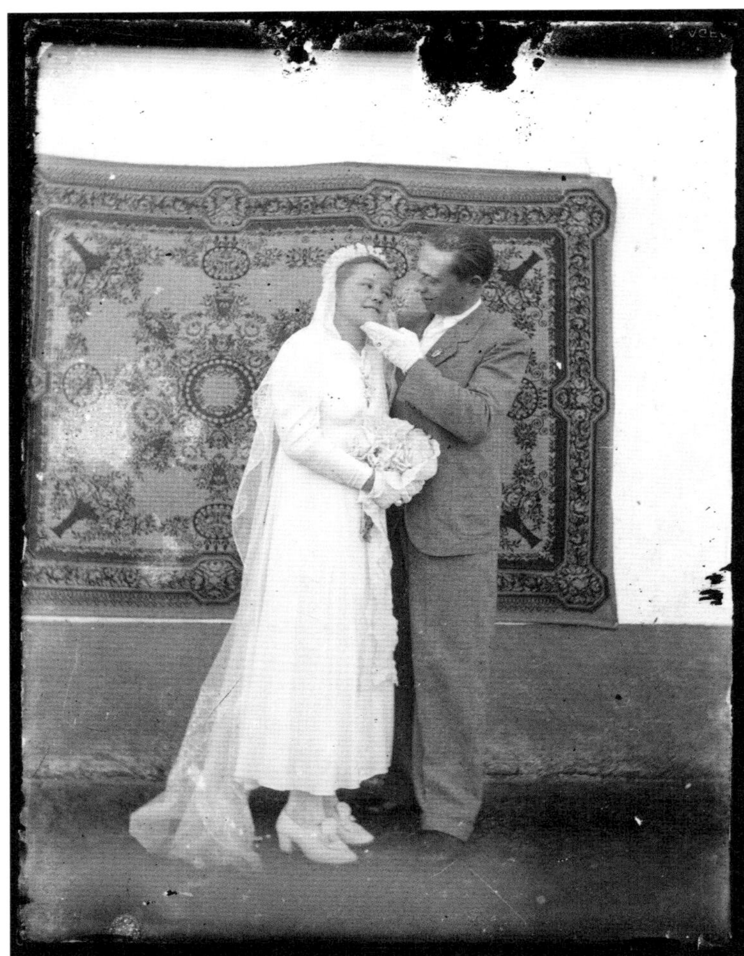

33

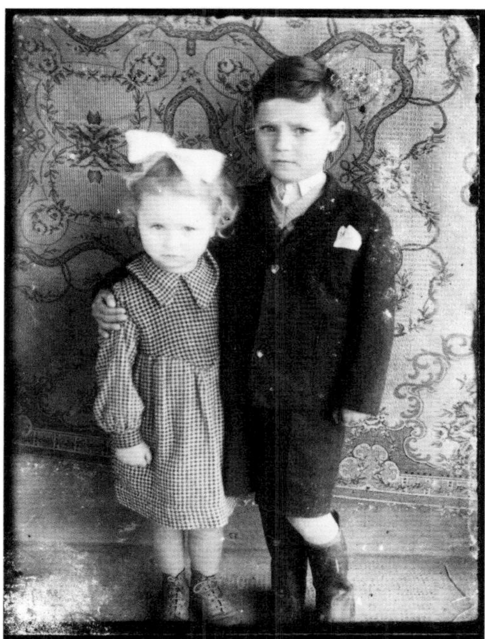

34

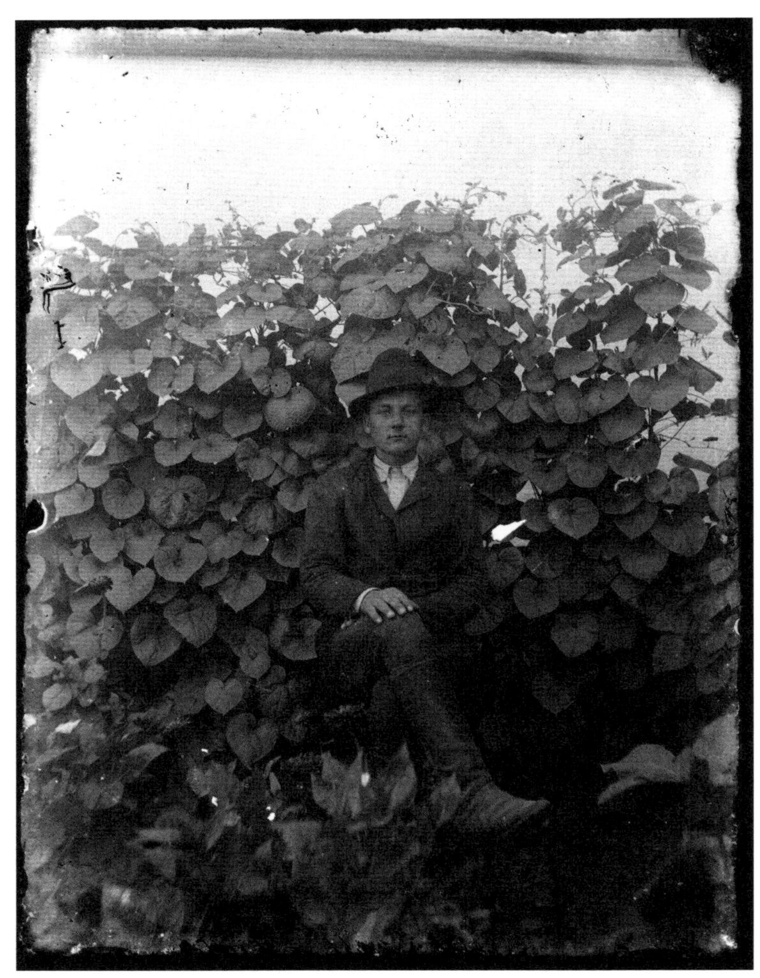

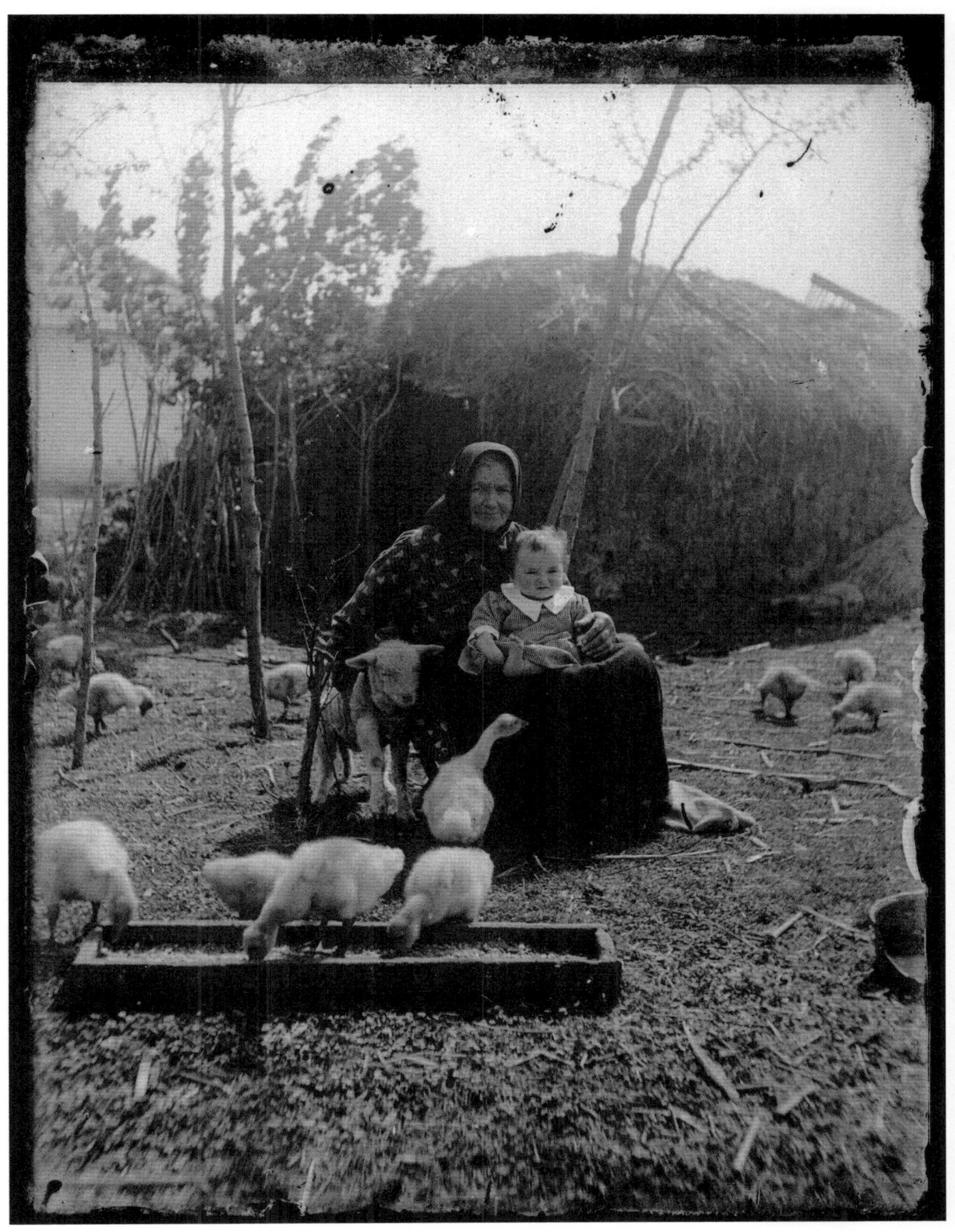

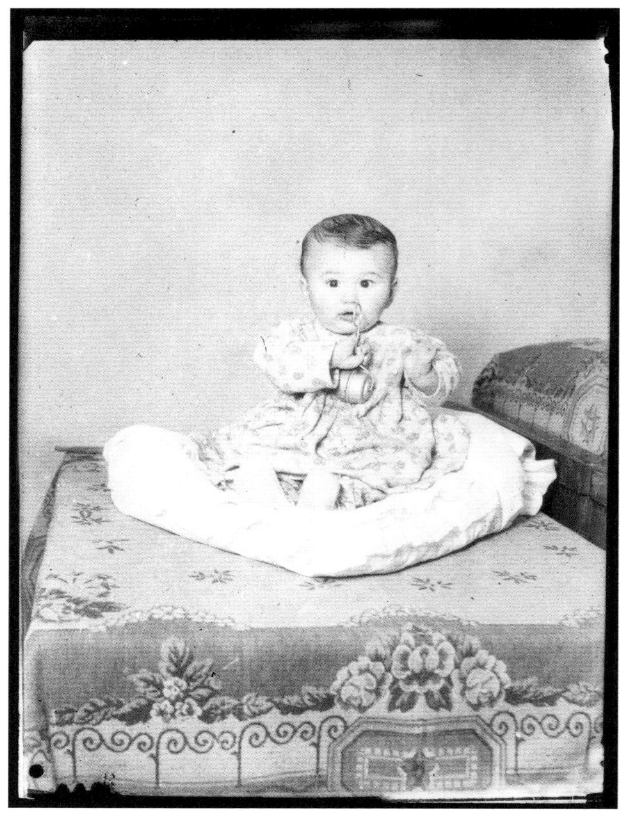

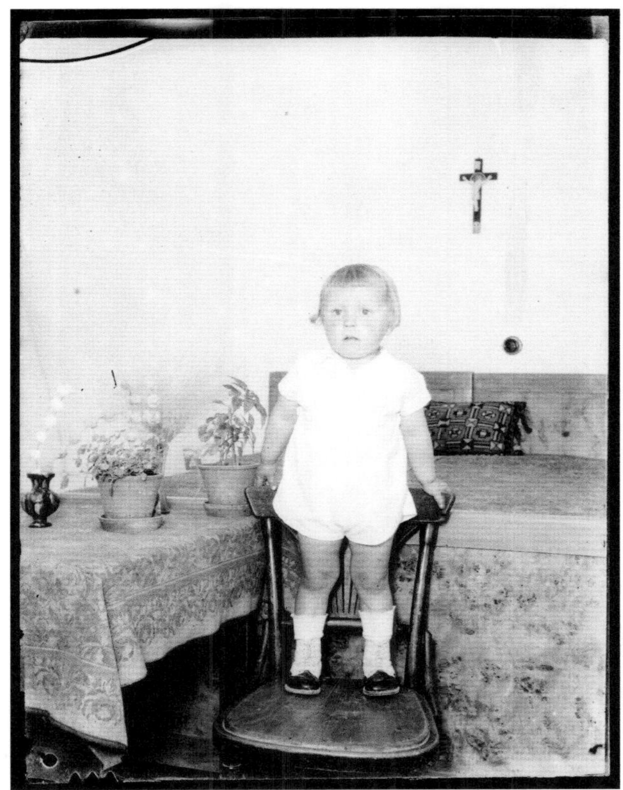

38

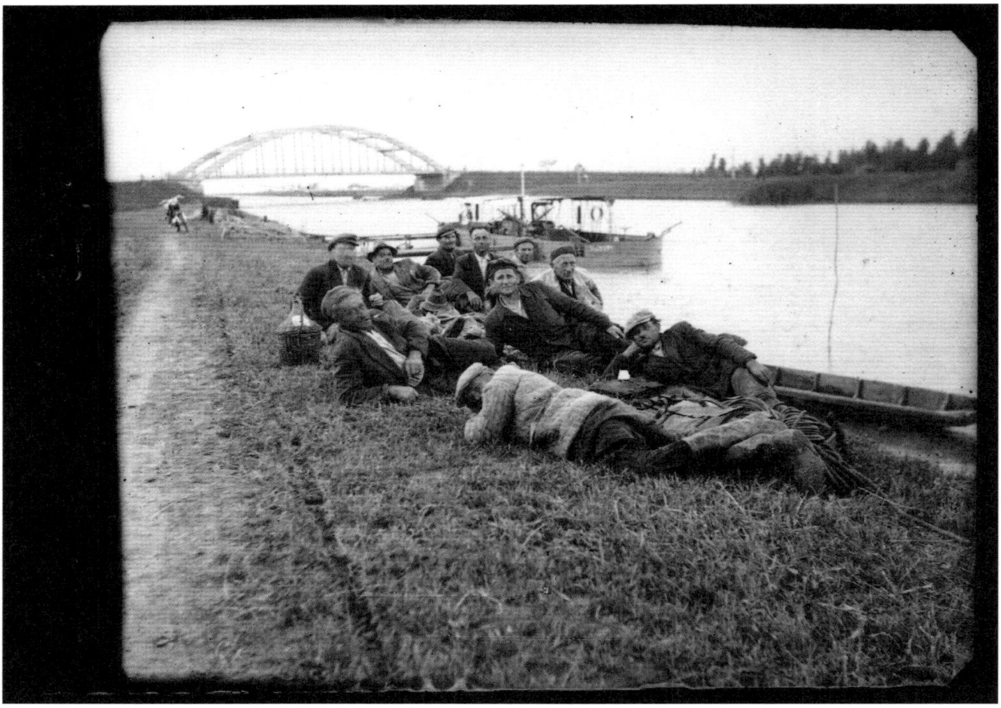

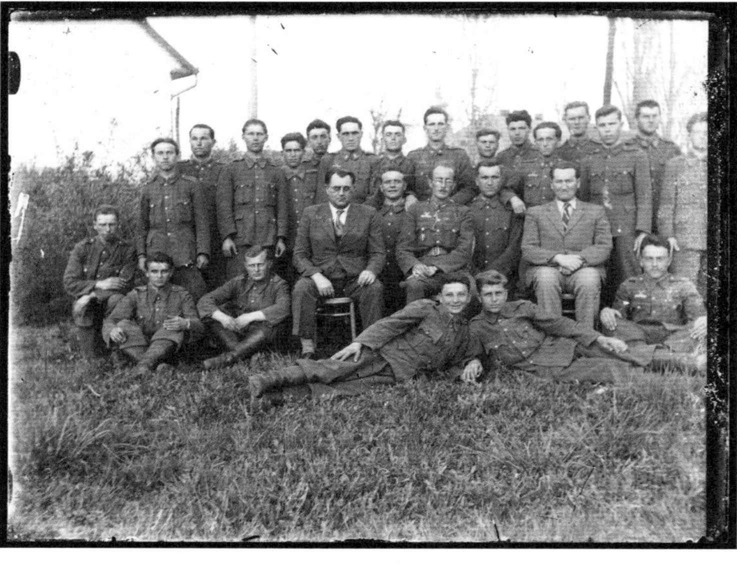

39

40

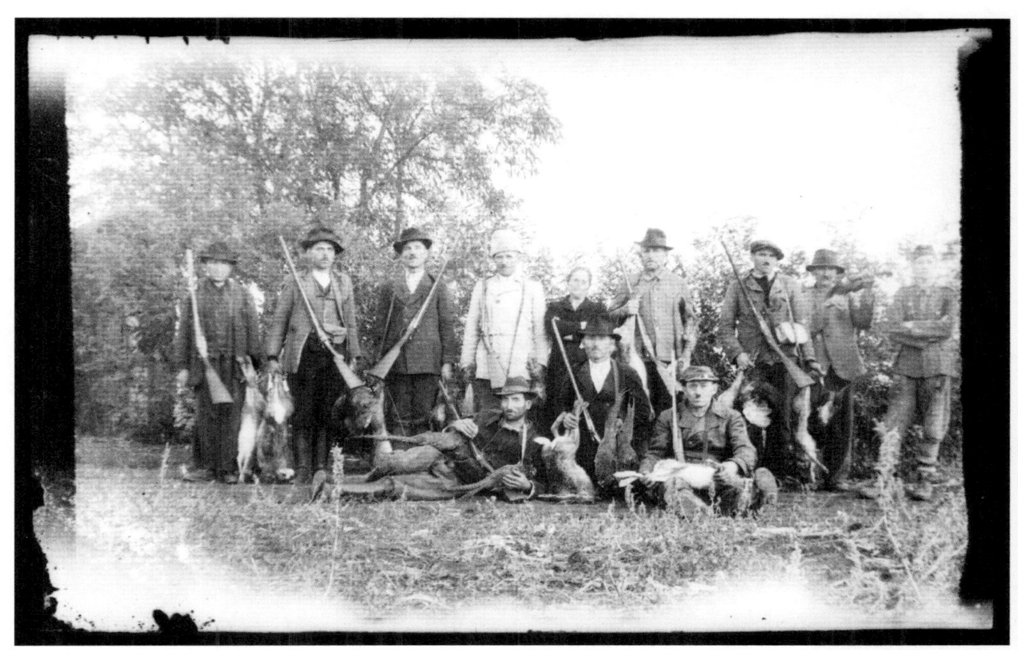

41

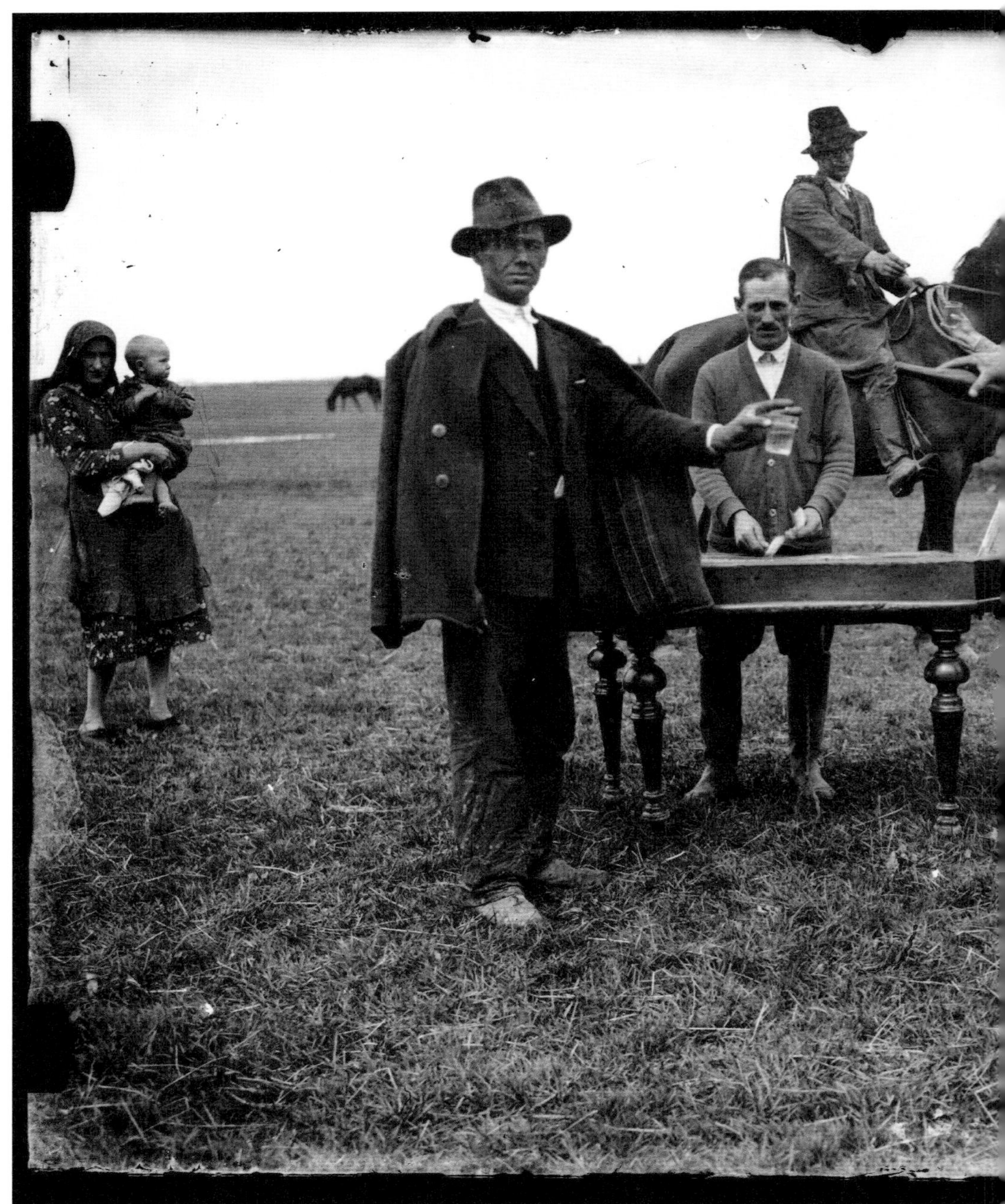

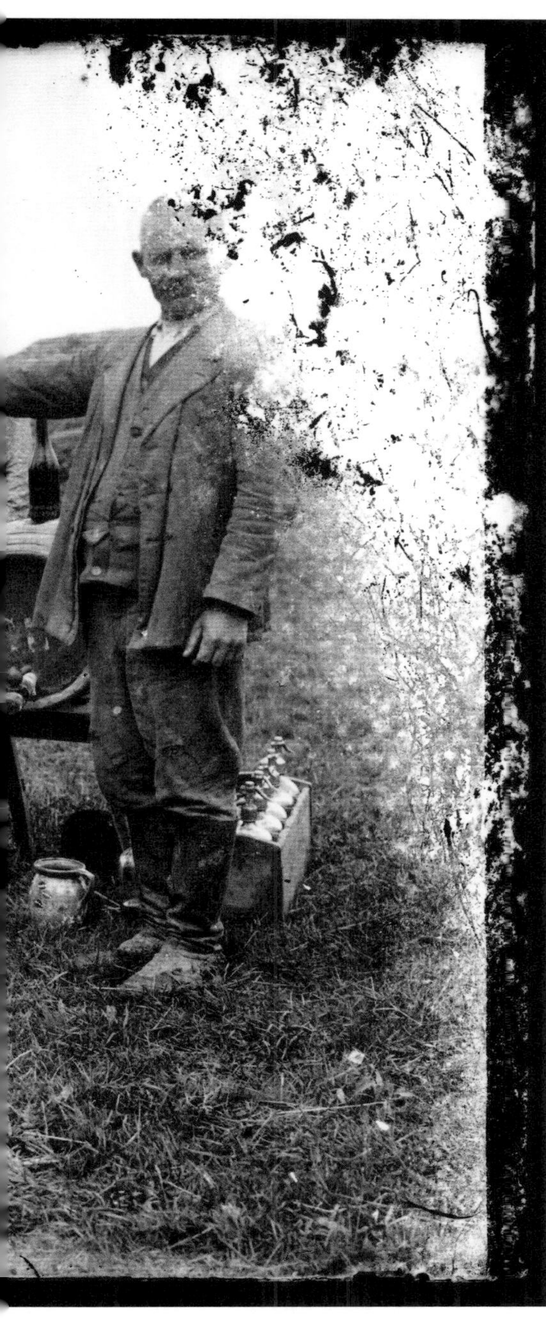

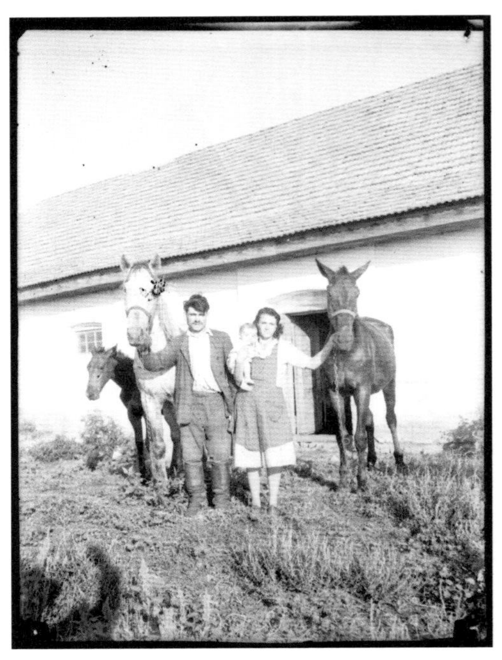

43

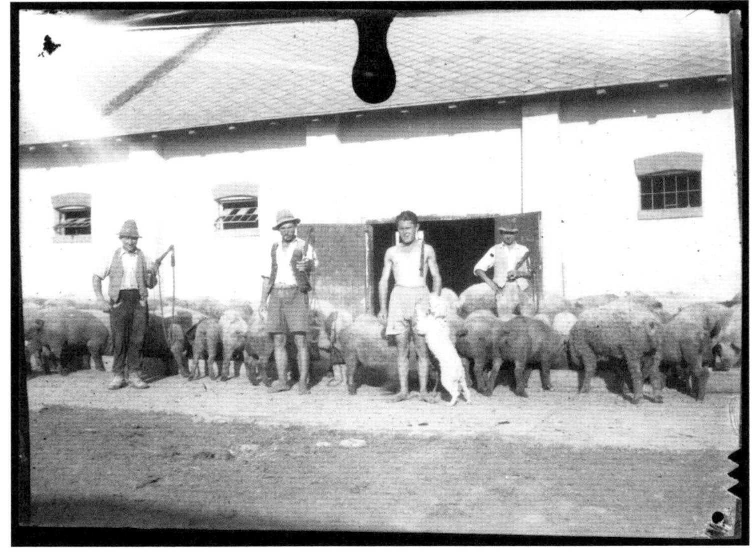

44

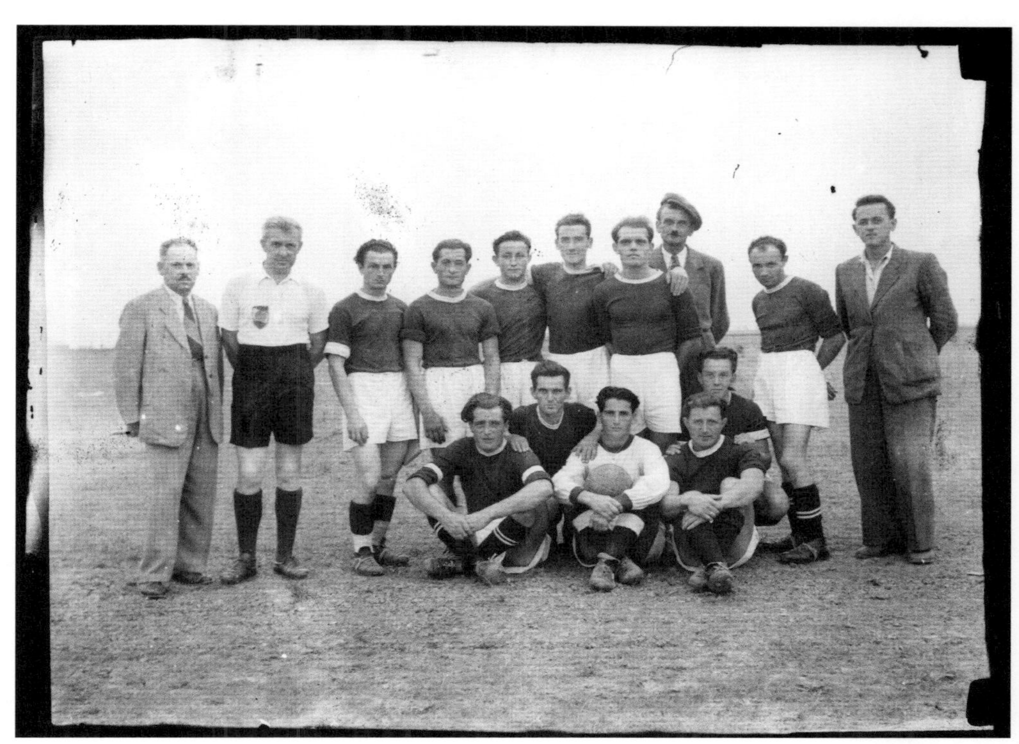

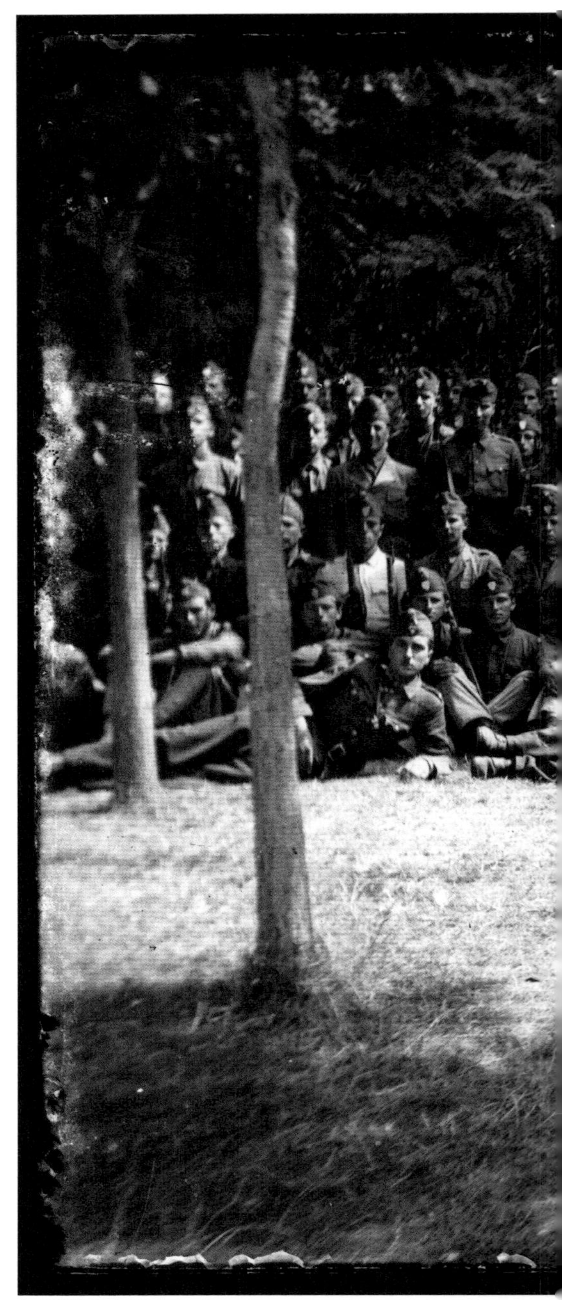

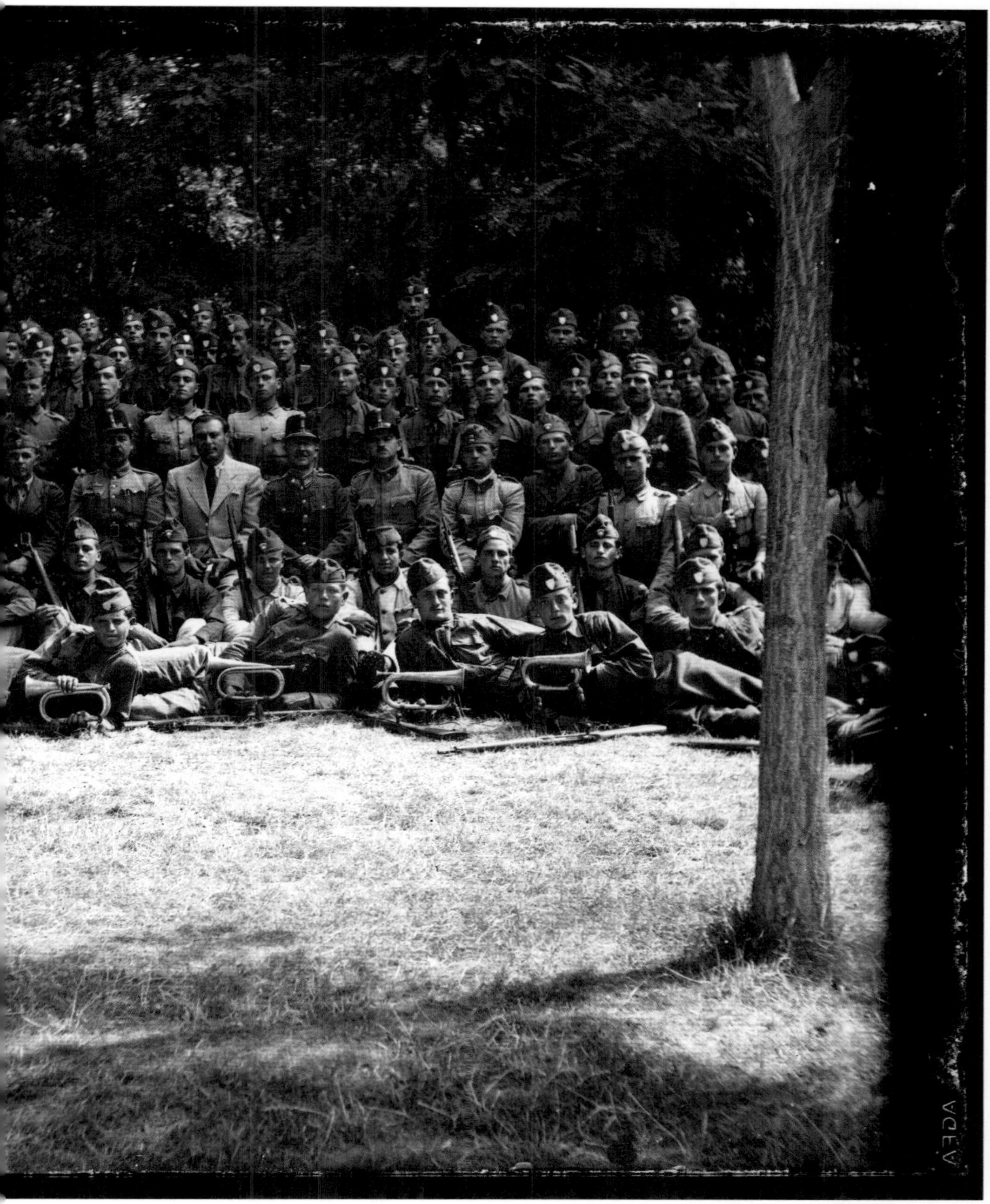

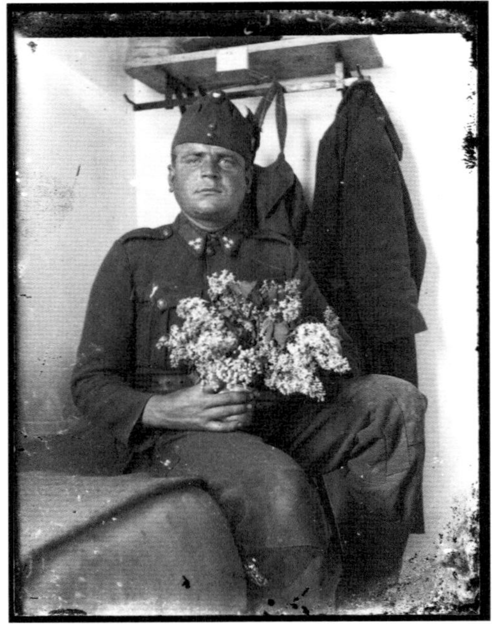

47

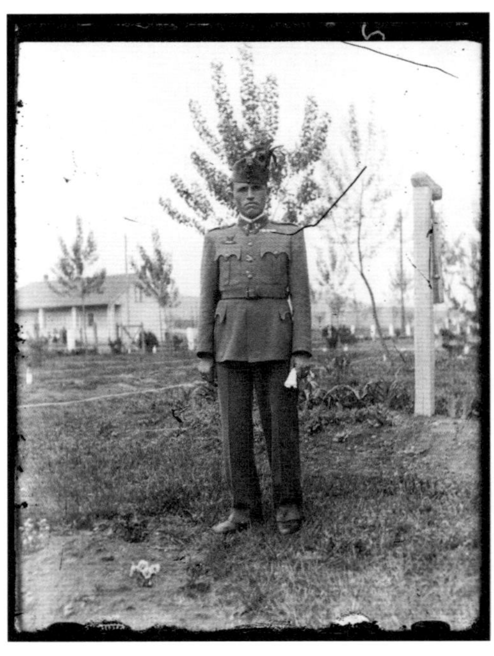

48

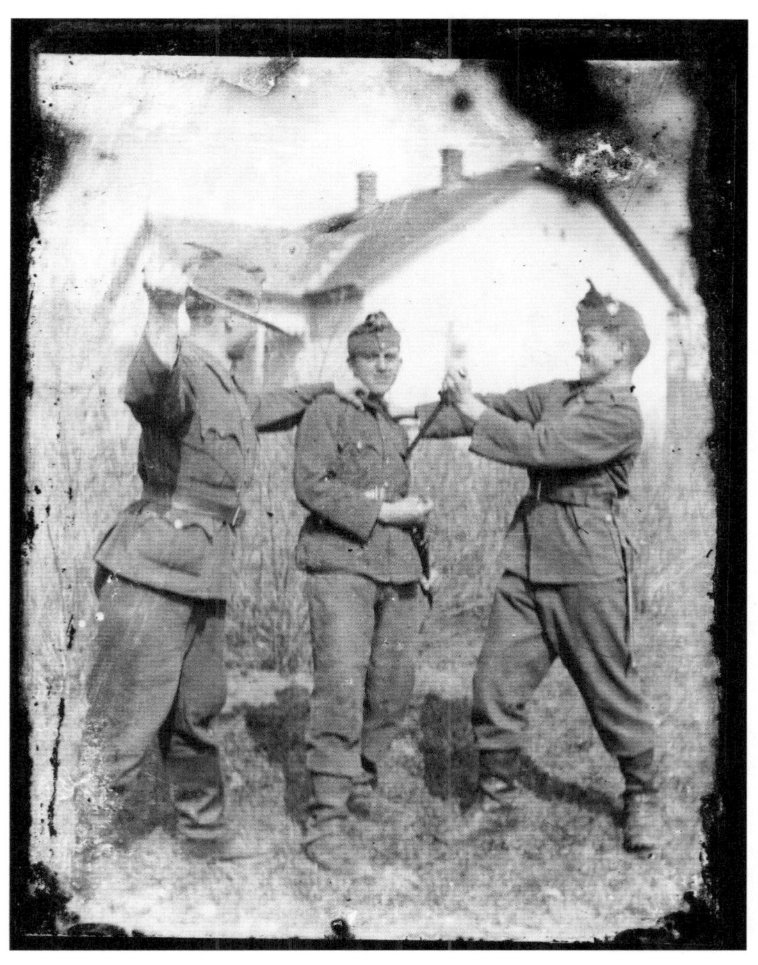

49

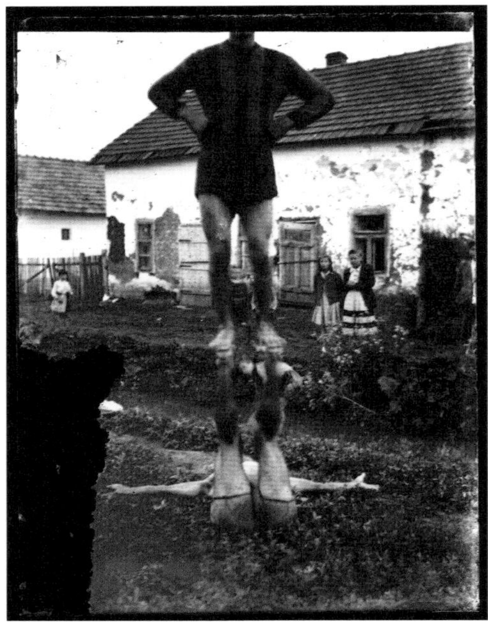

50

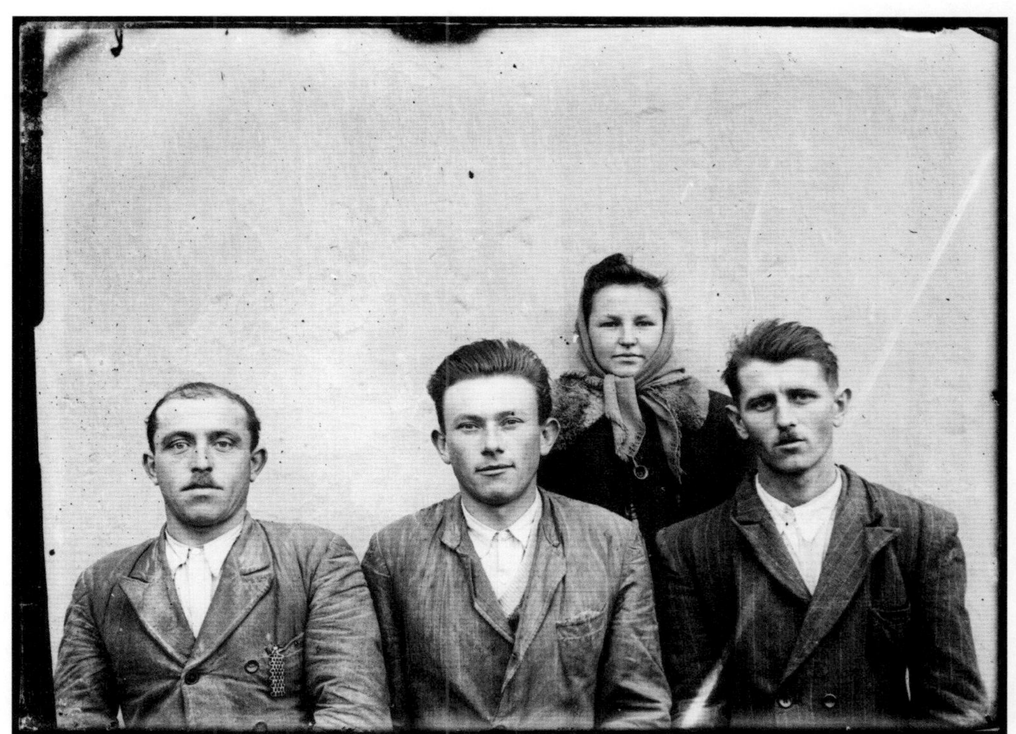

51

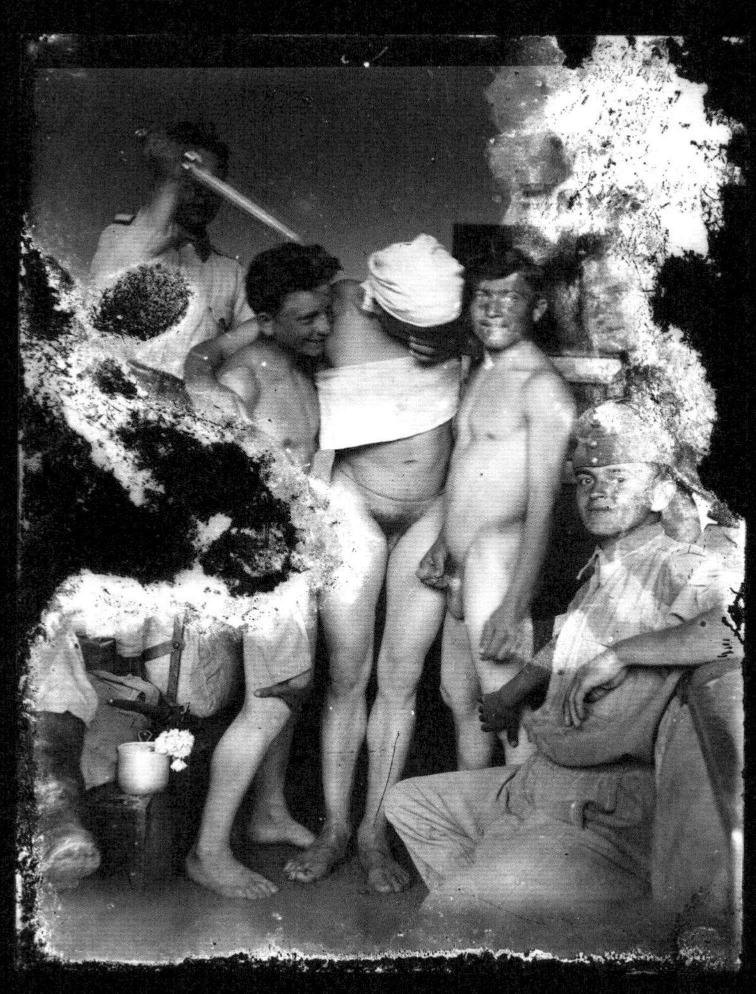

52

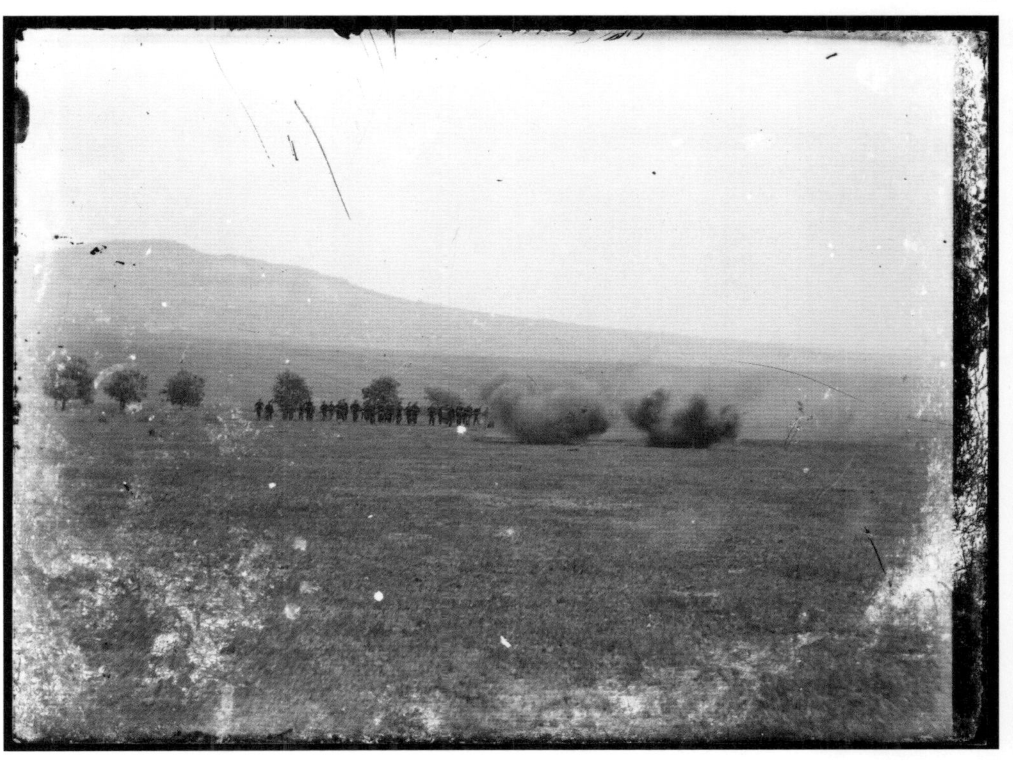

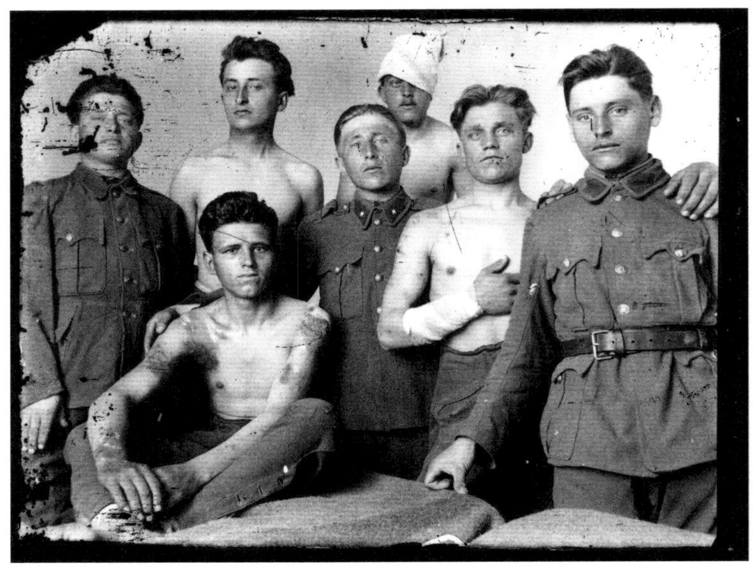

54

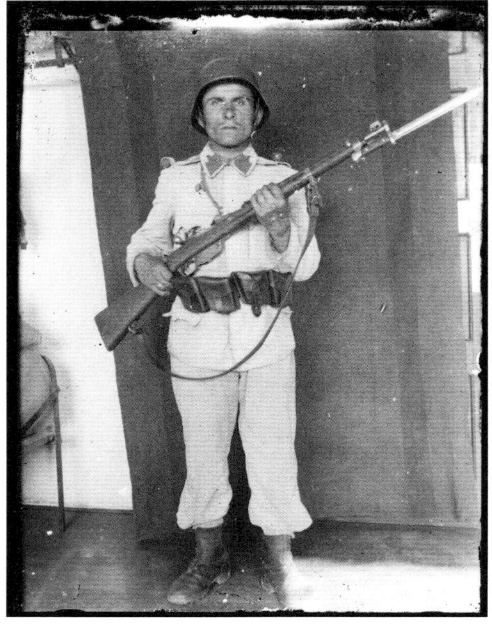

55

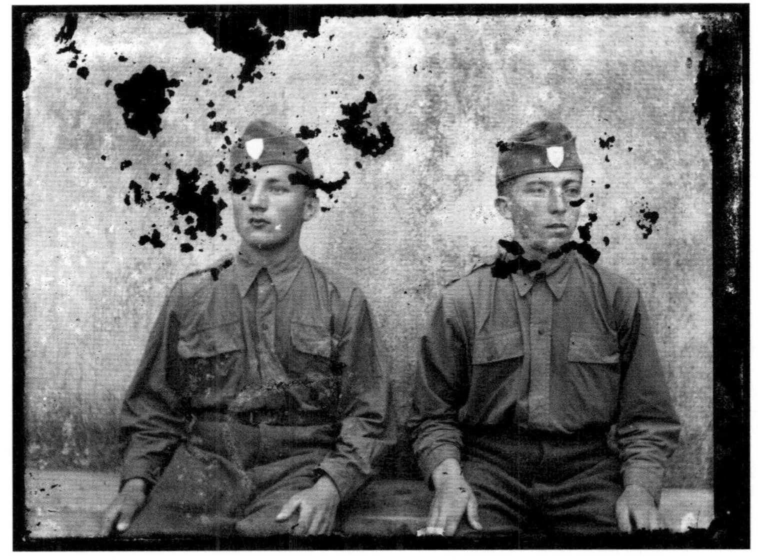

56

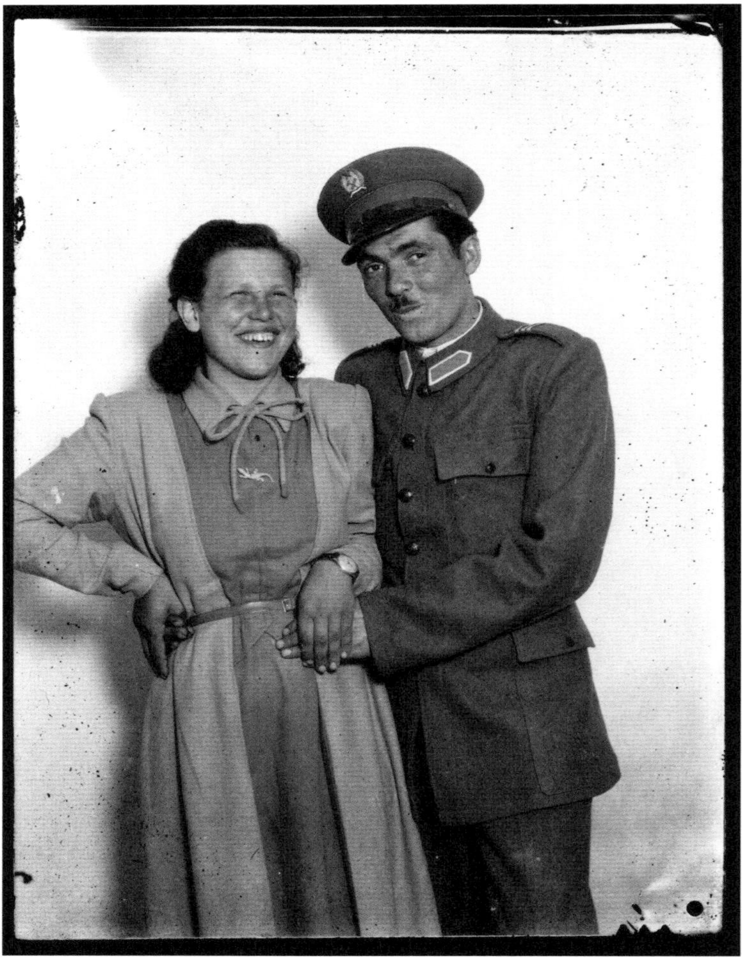

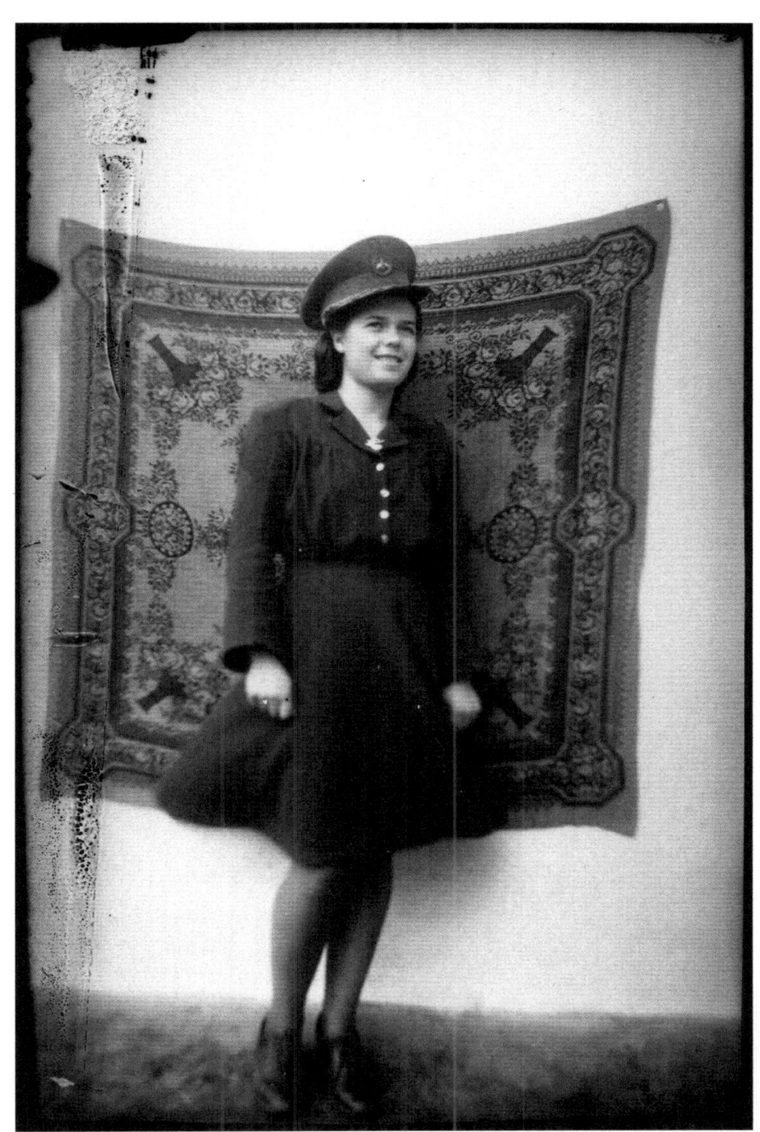

58

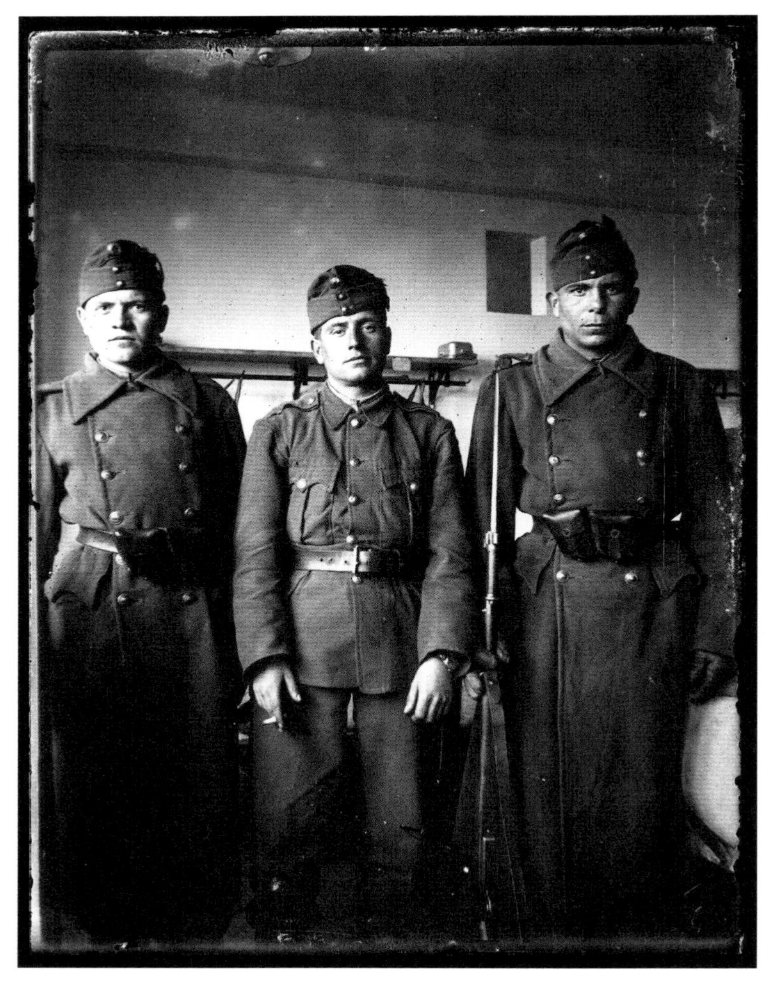

59

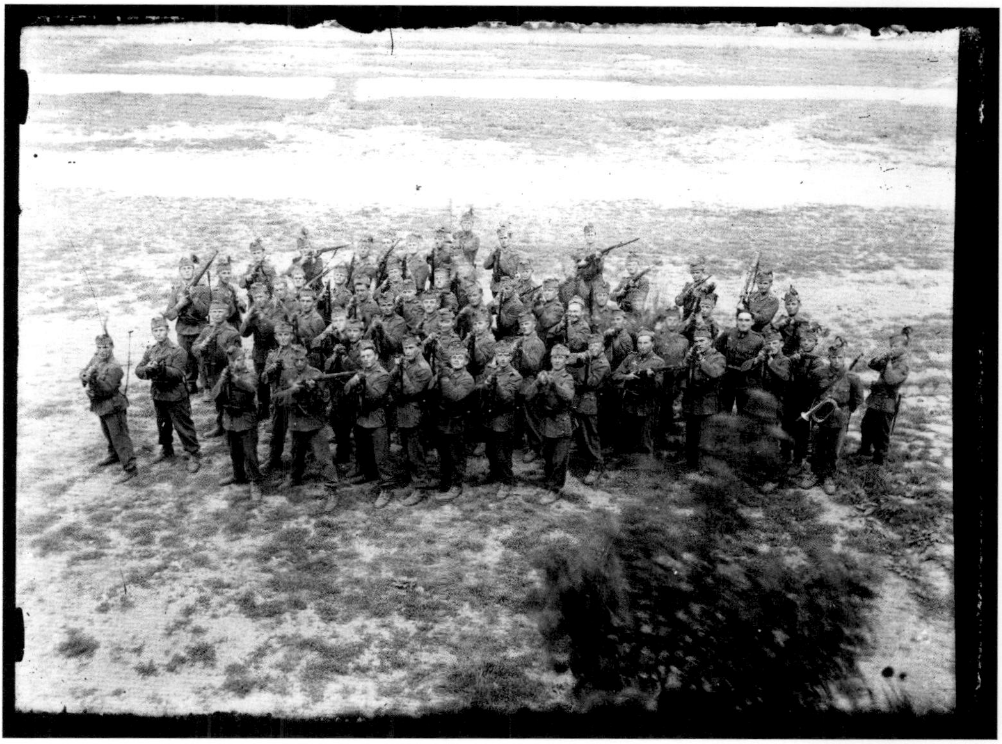

60

61

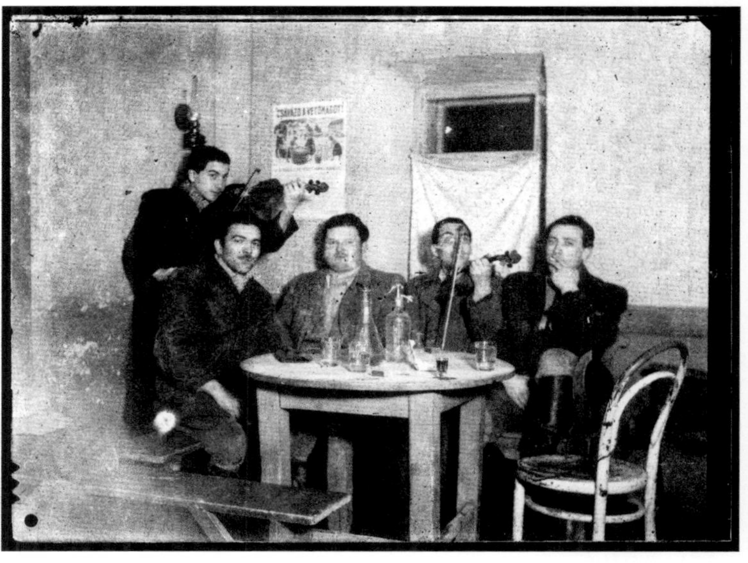

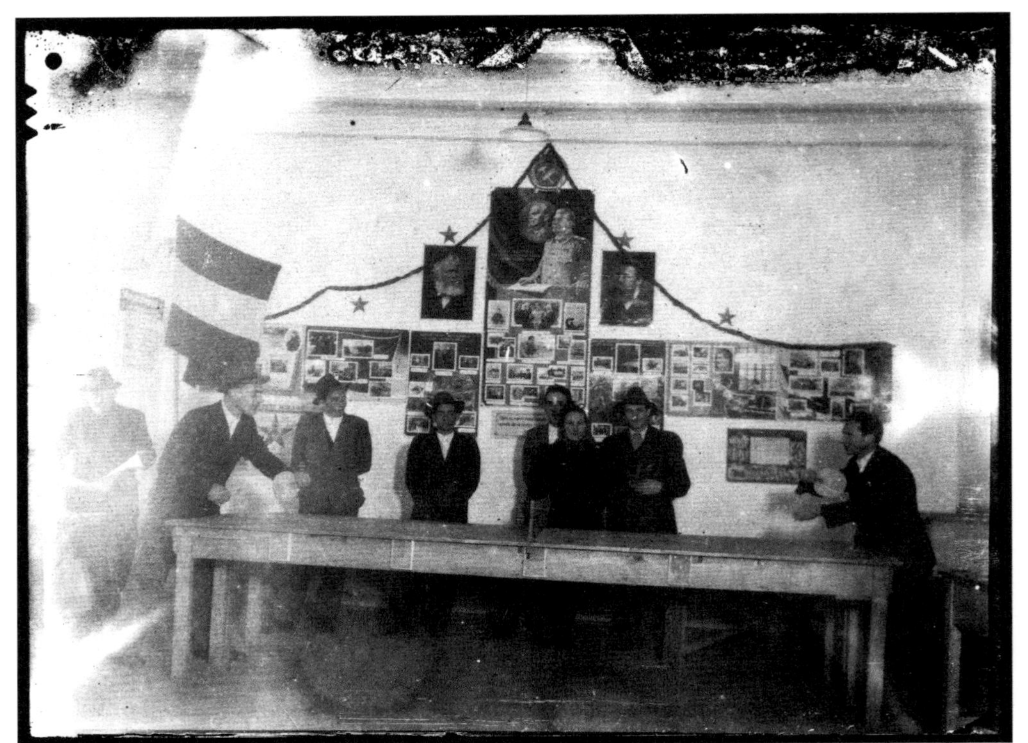

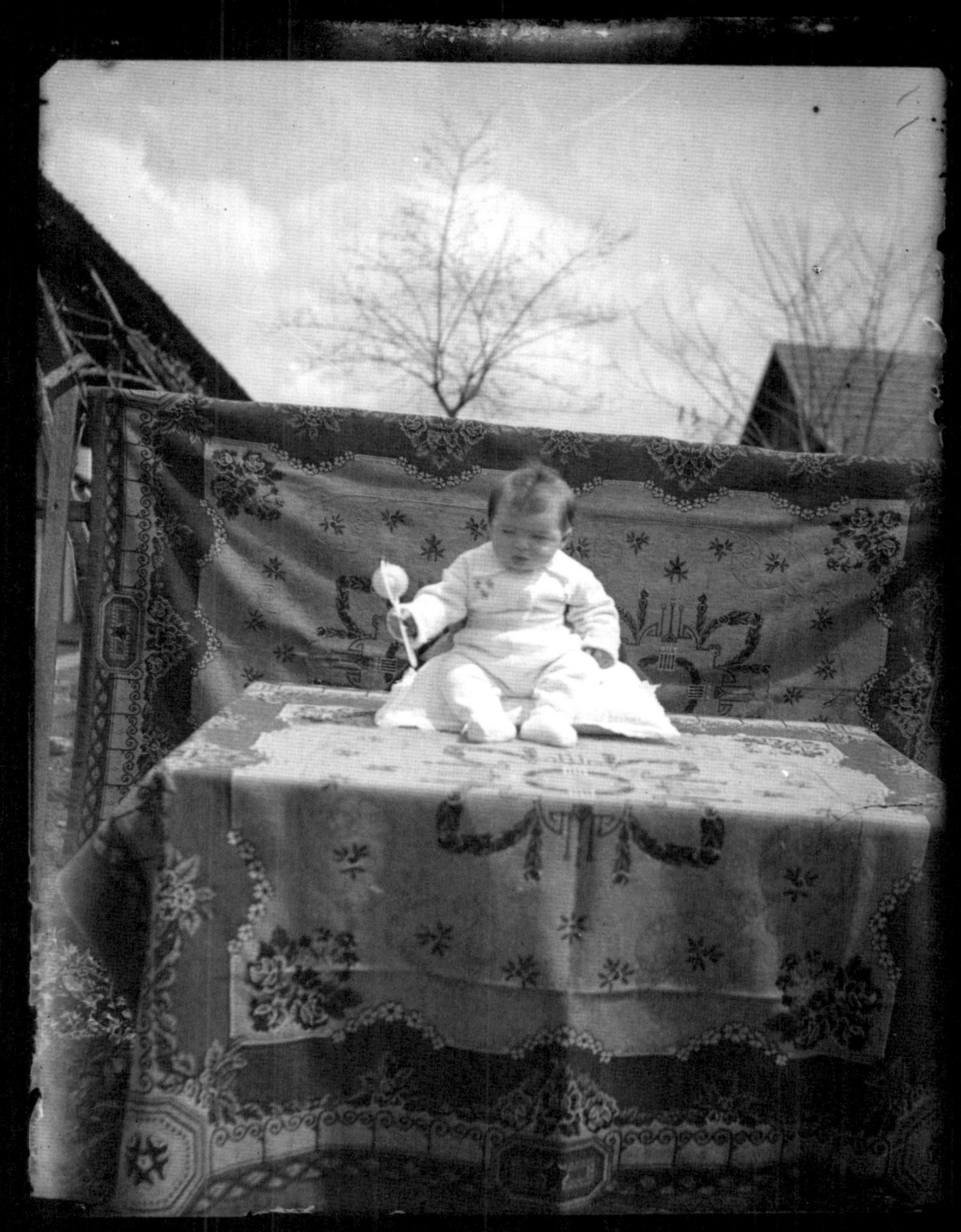

63

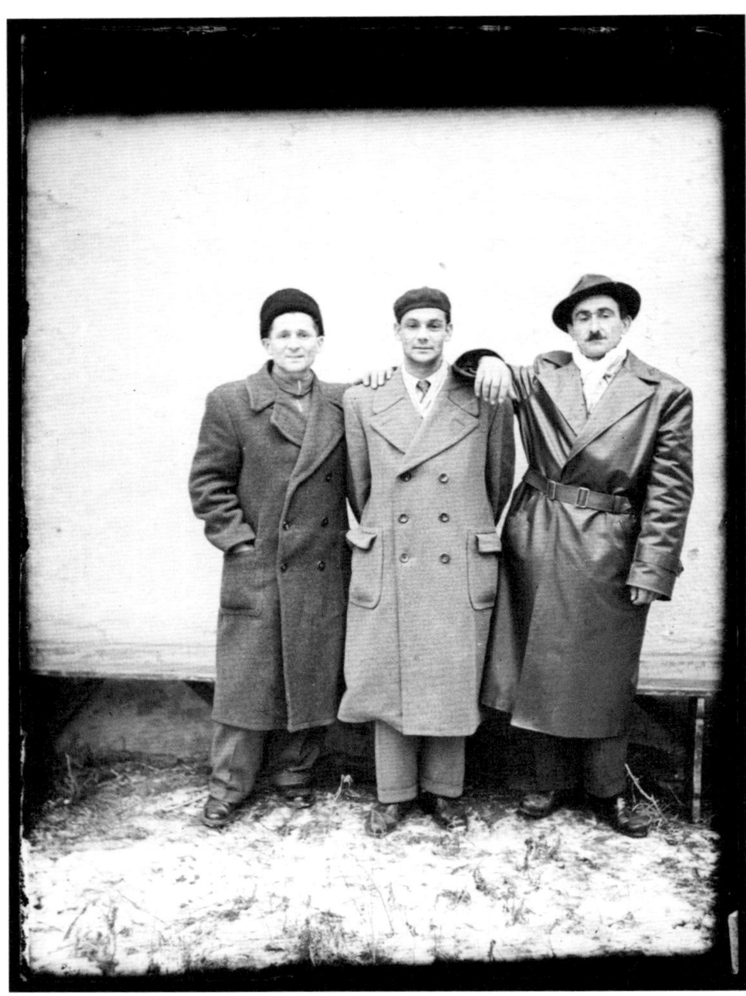

64

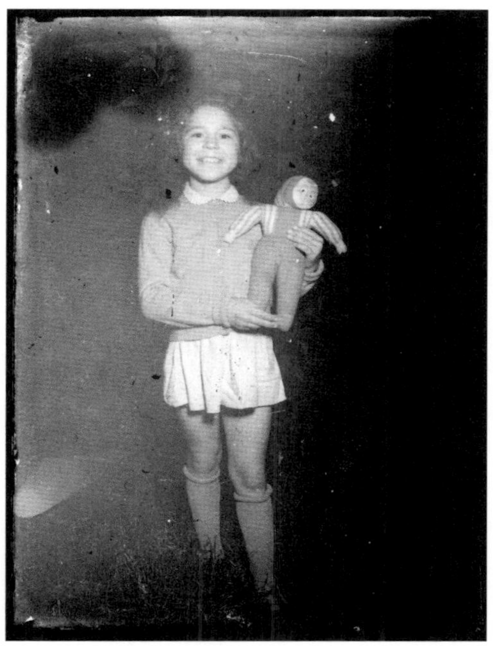

65

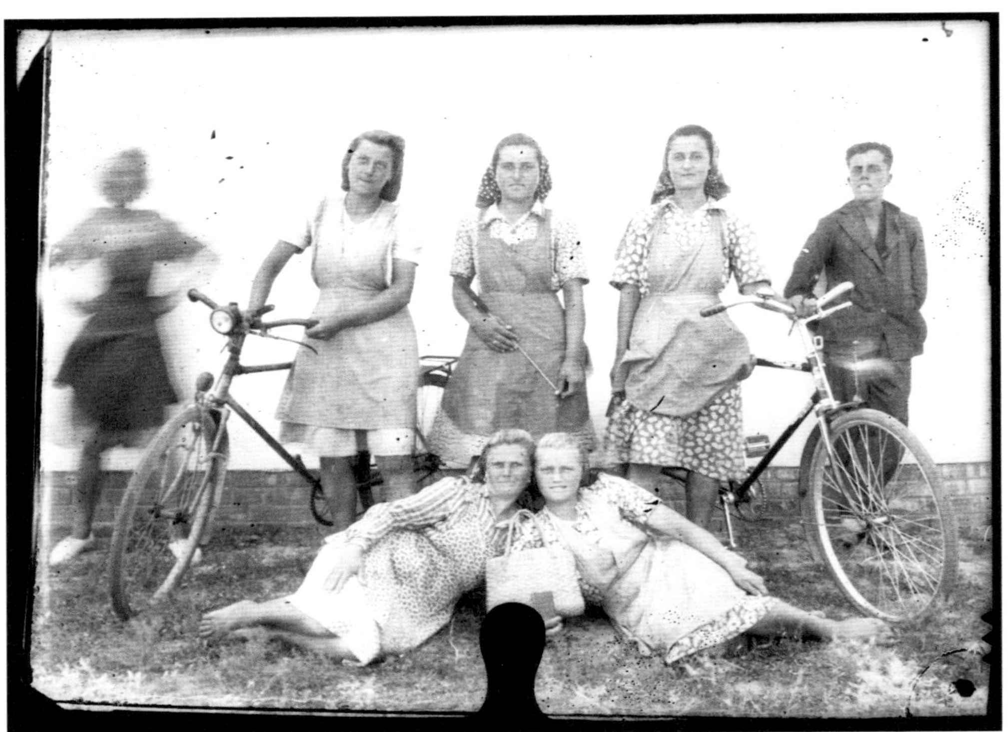

66

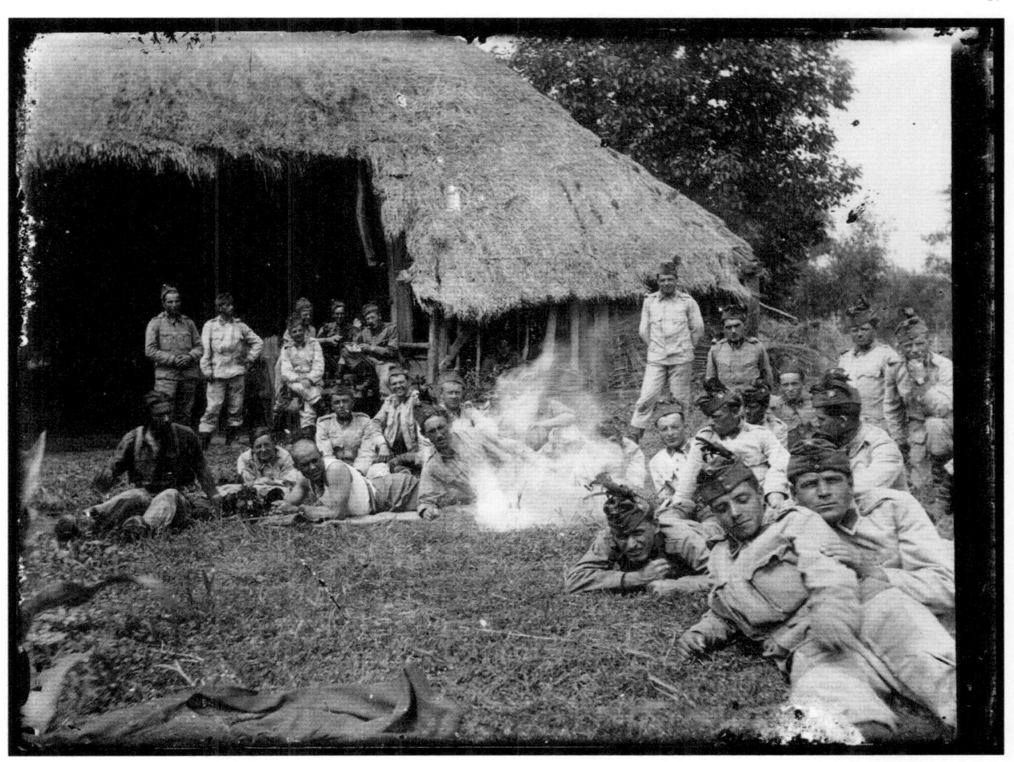

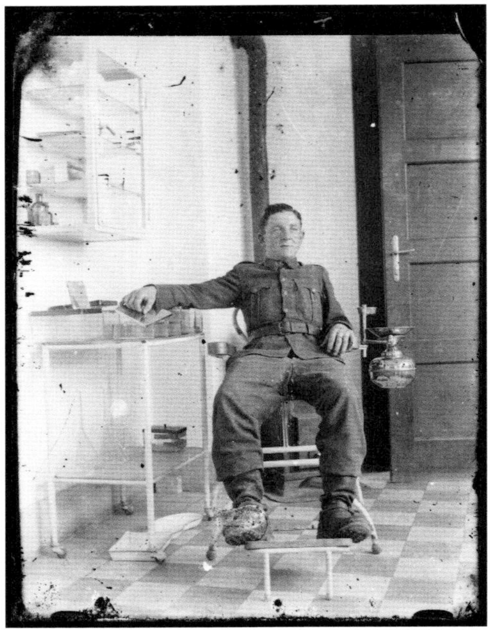

68

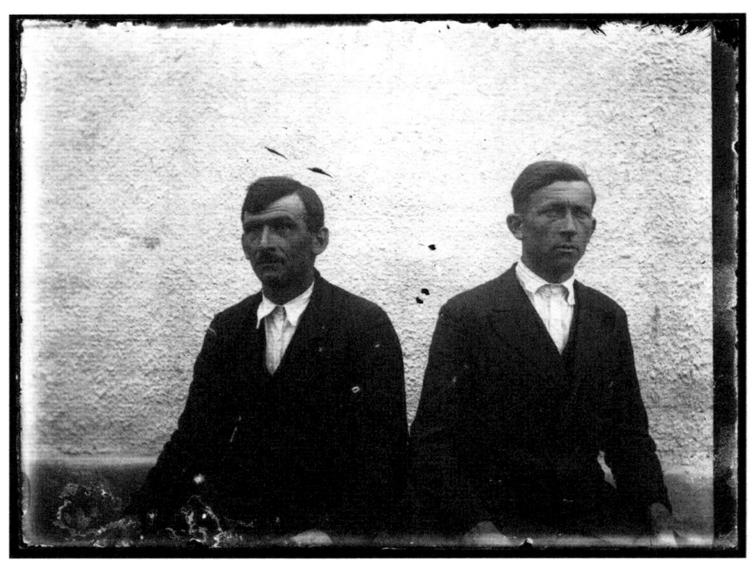

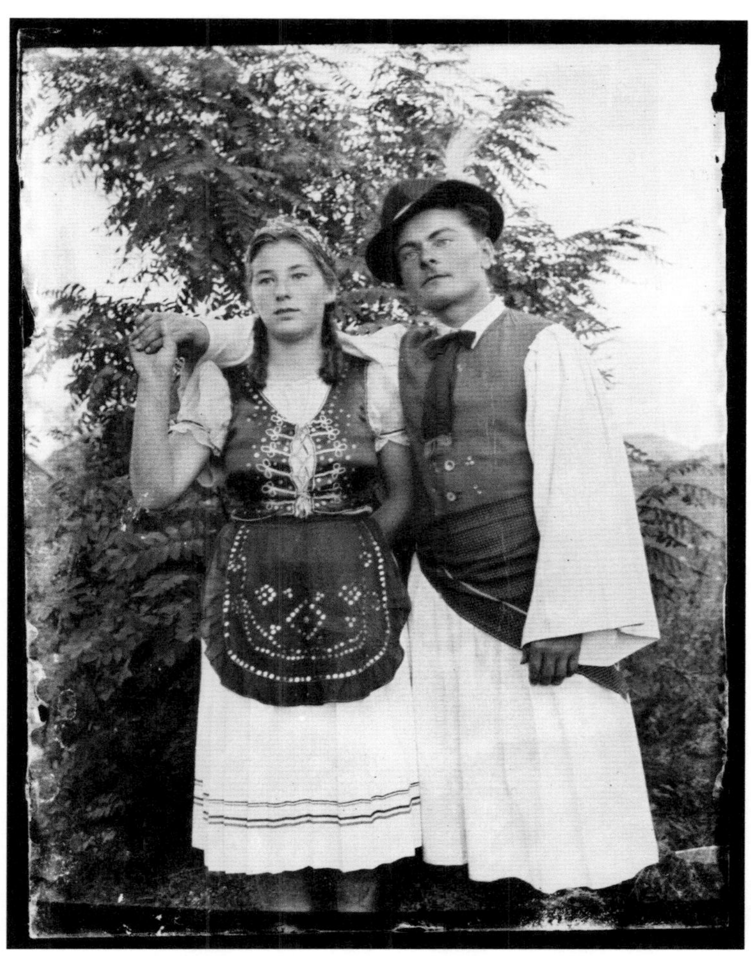

70

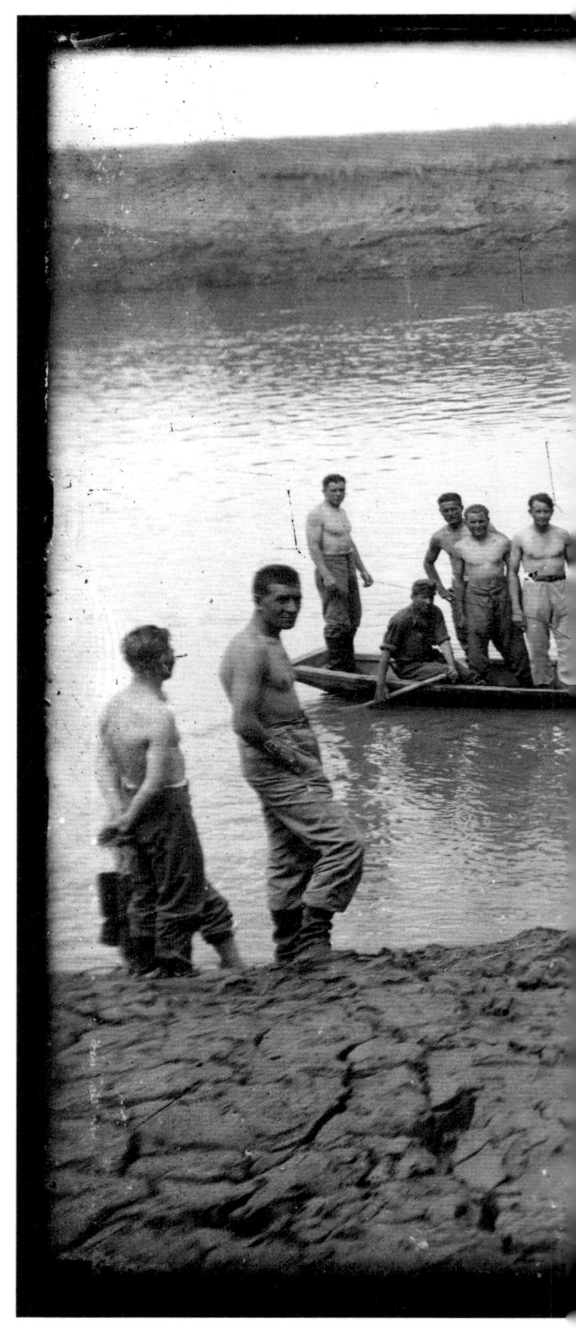

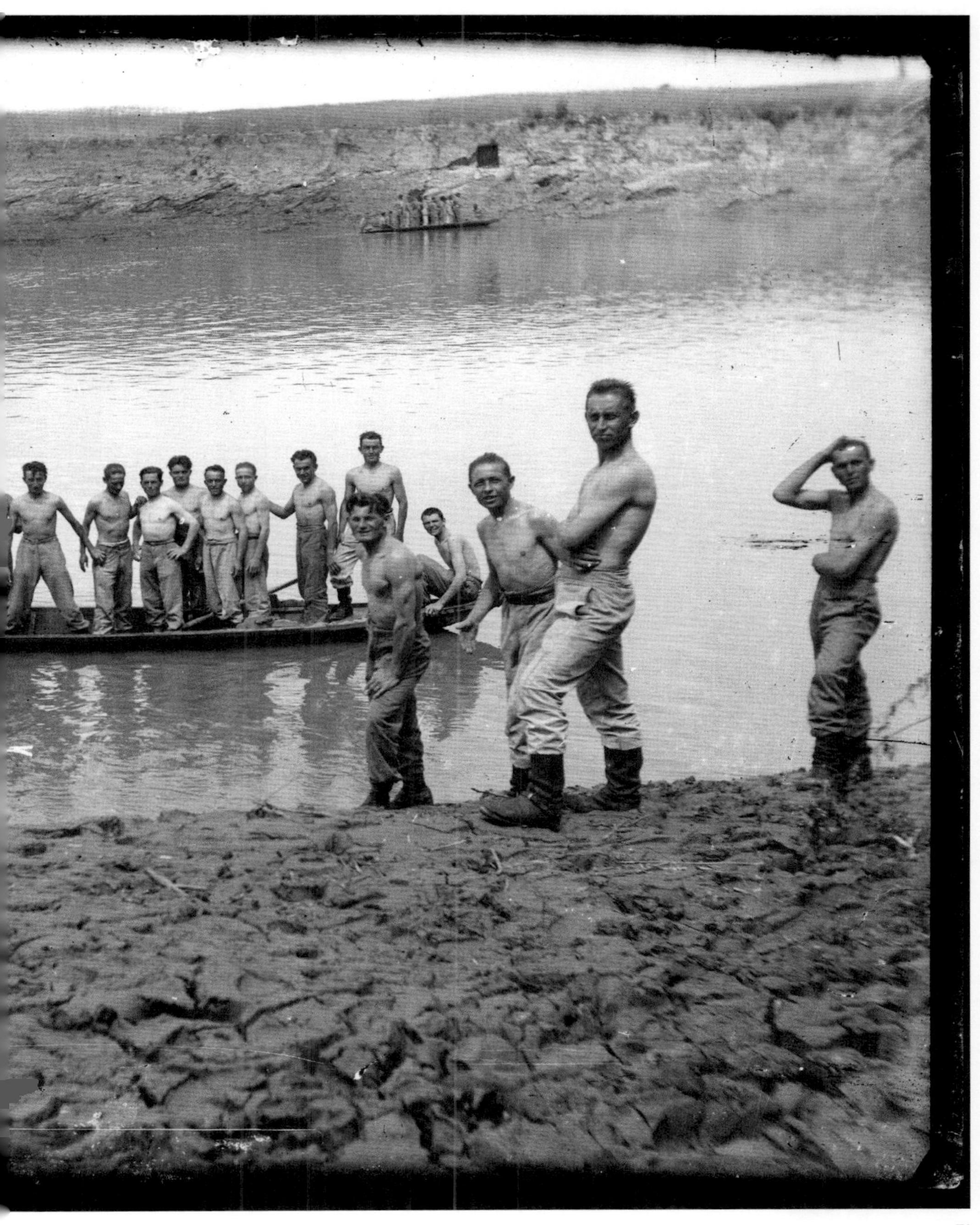

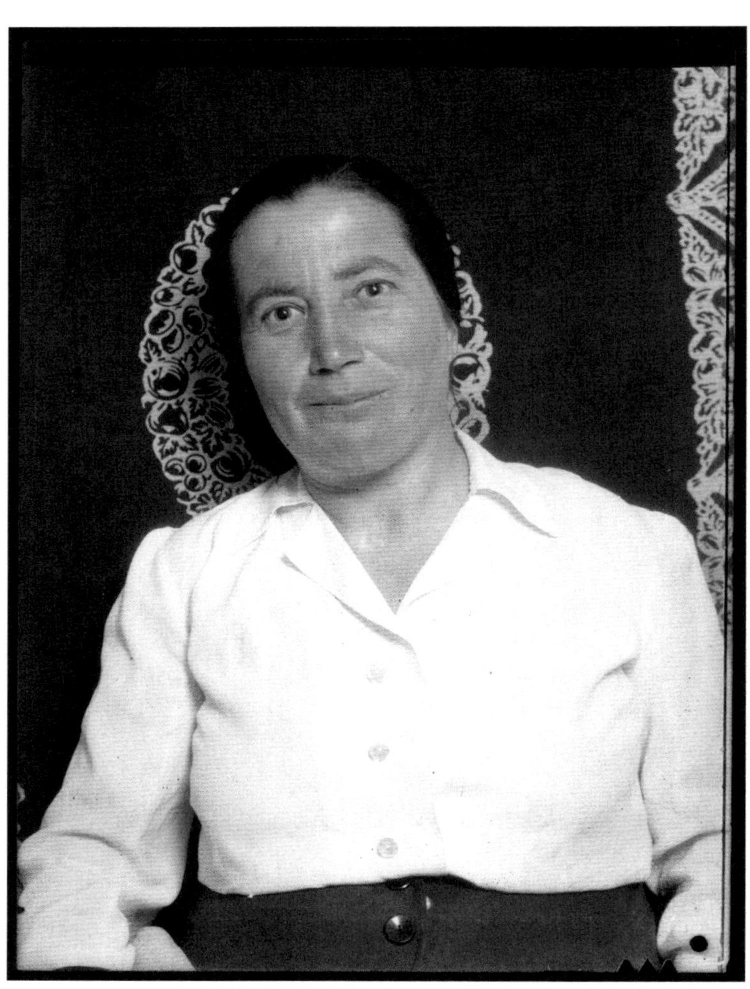

72

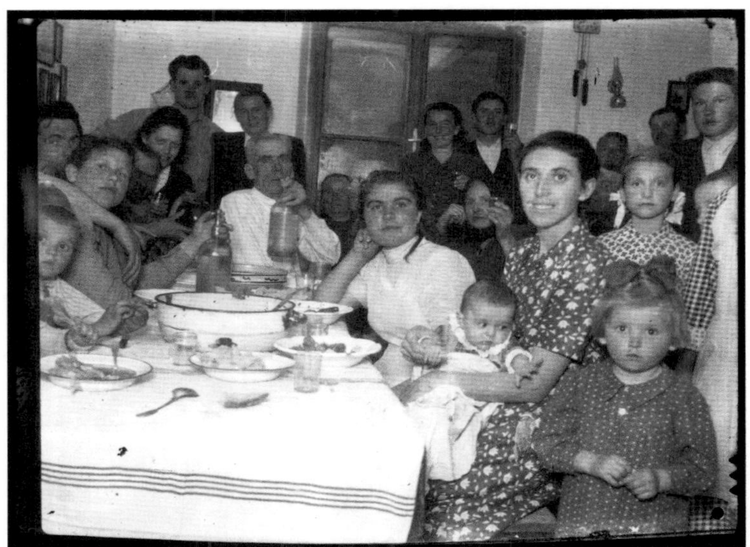

73

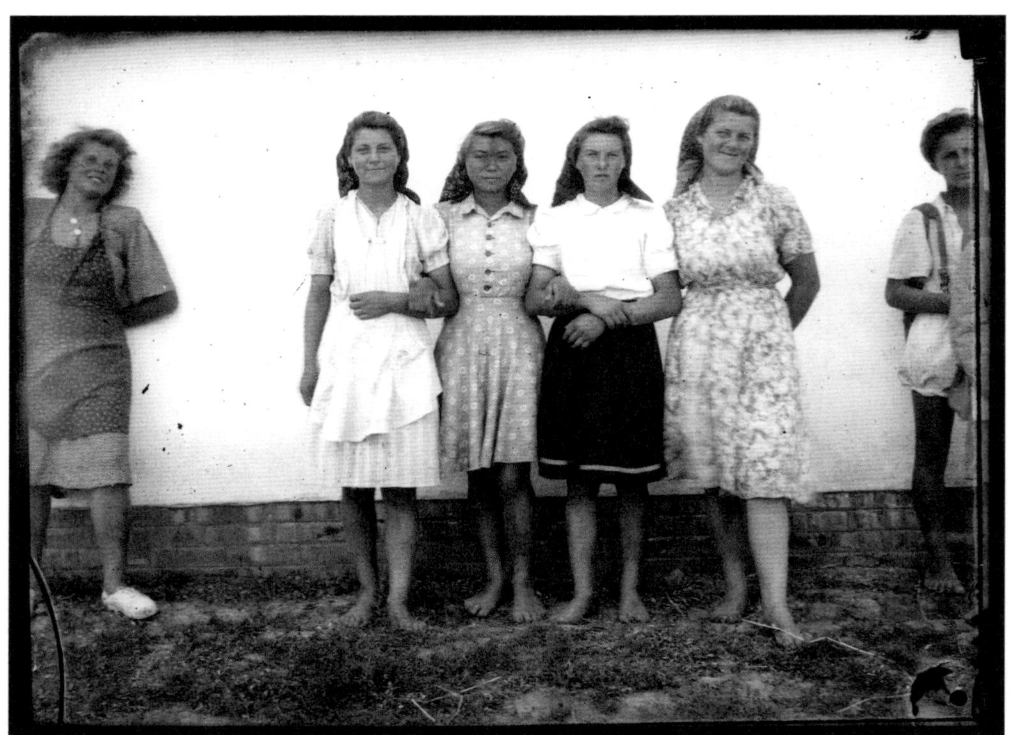

74

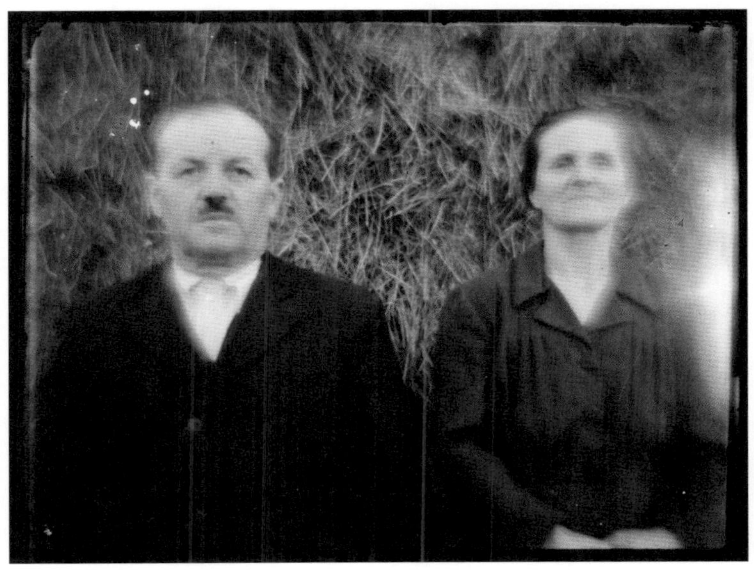

75

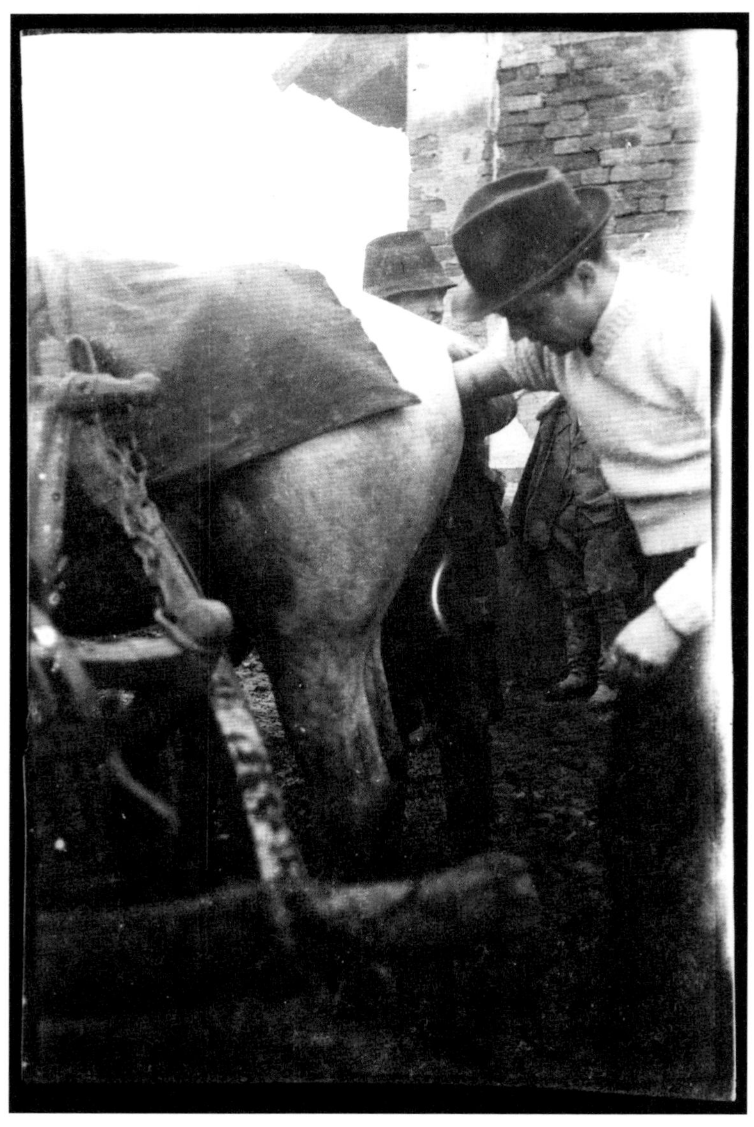

76

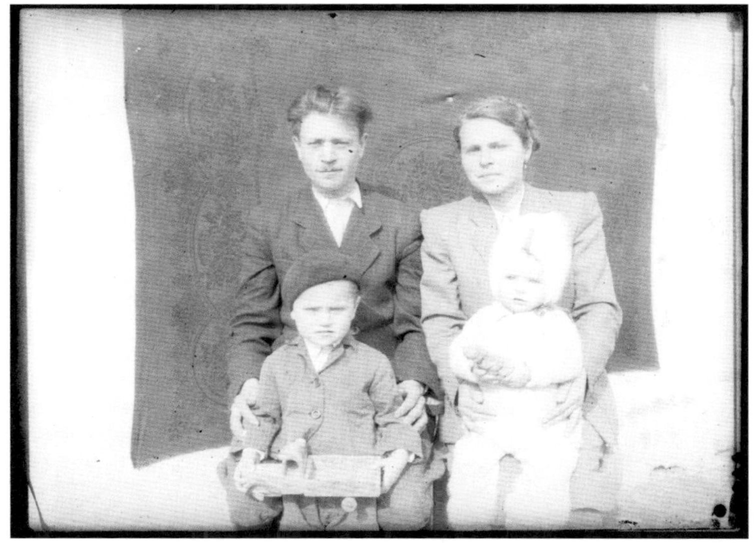

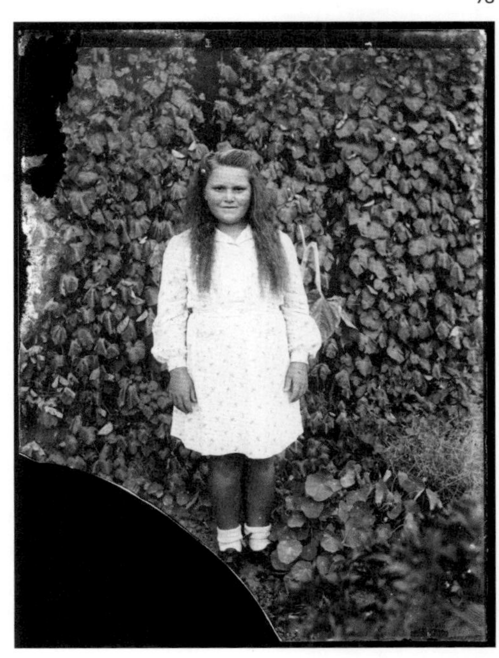

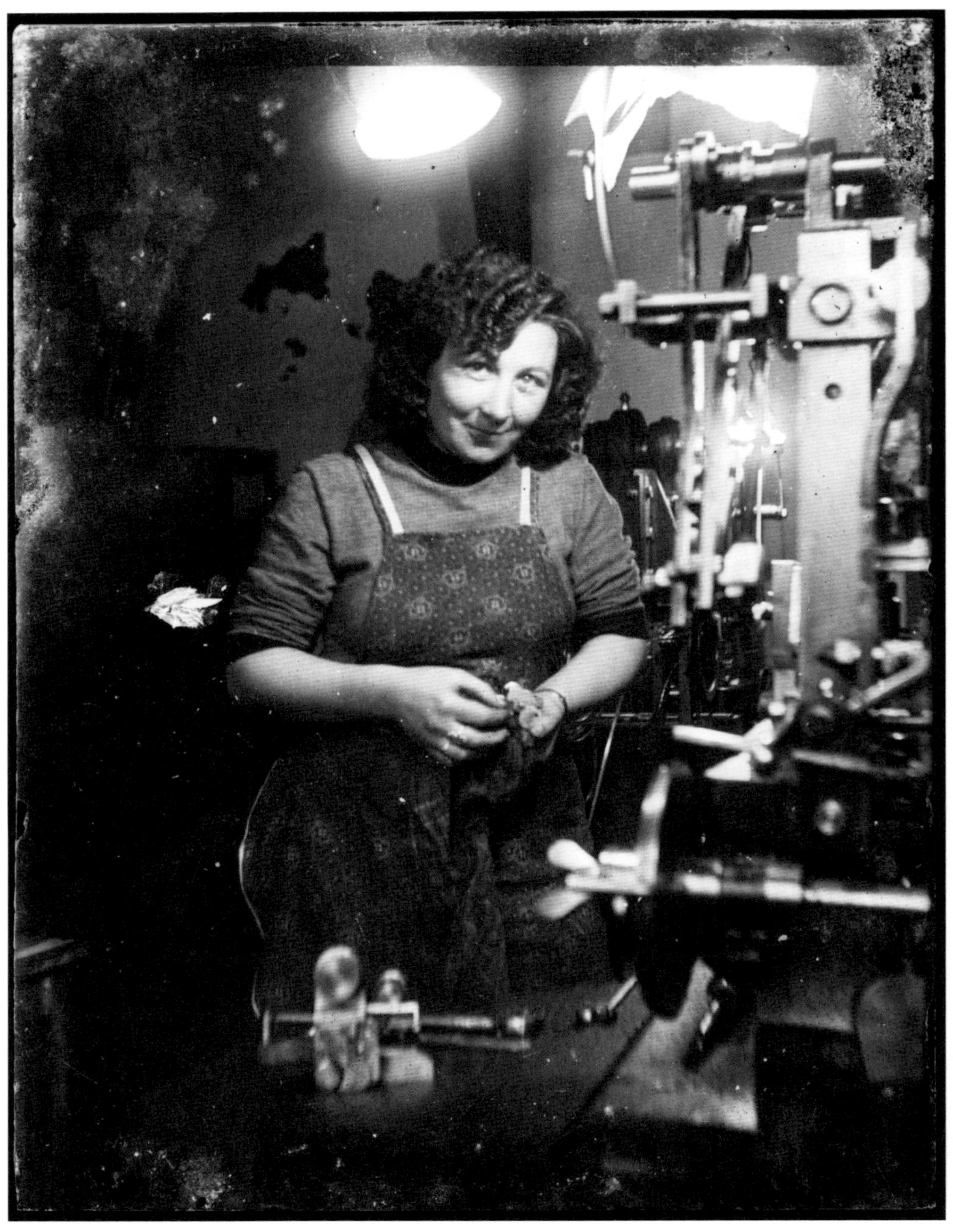

79

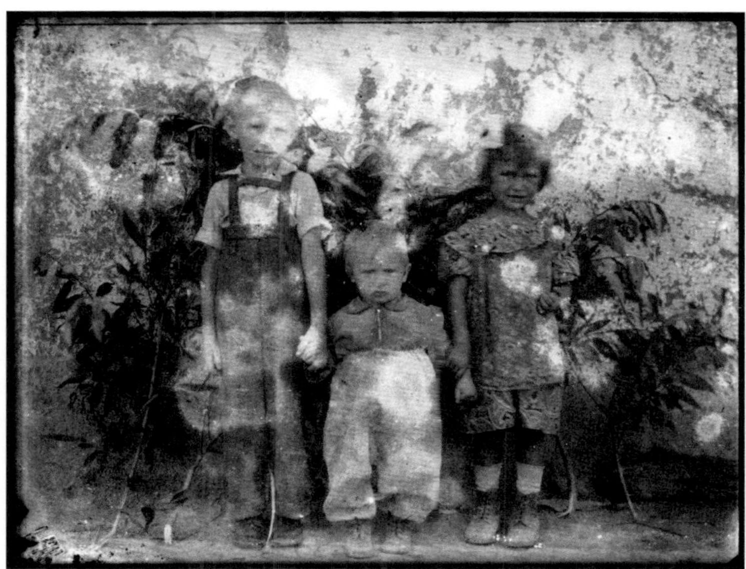

80

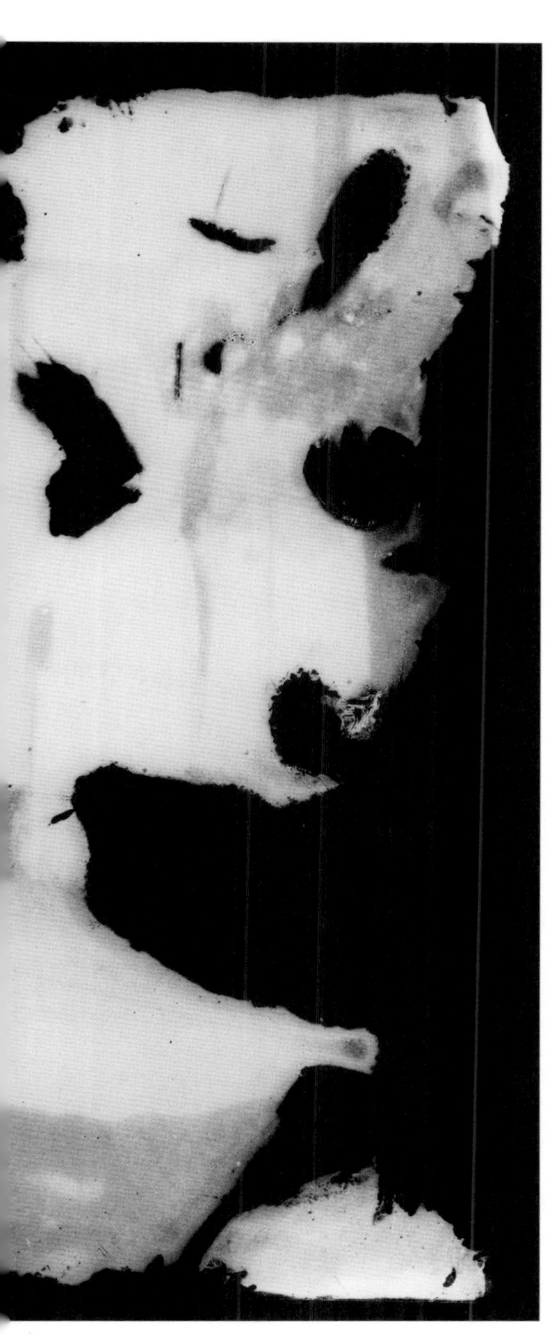

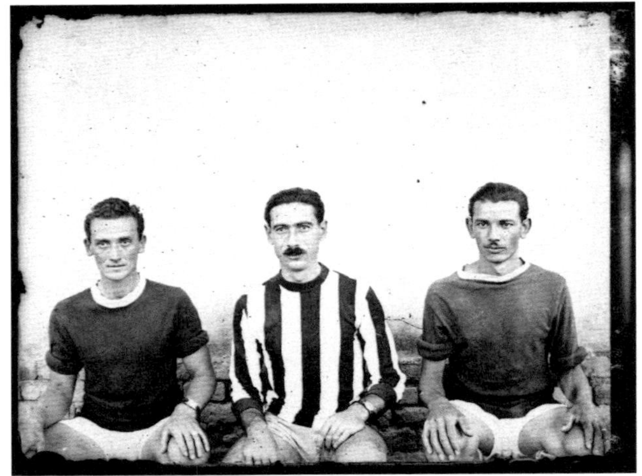

82

83

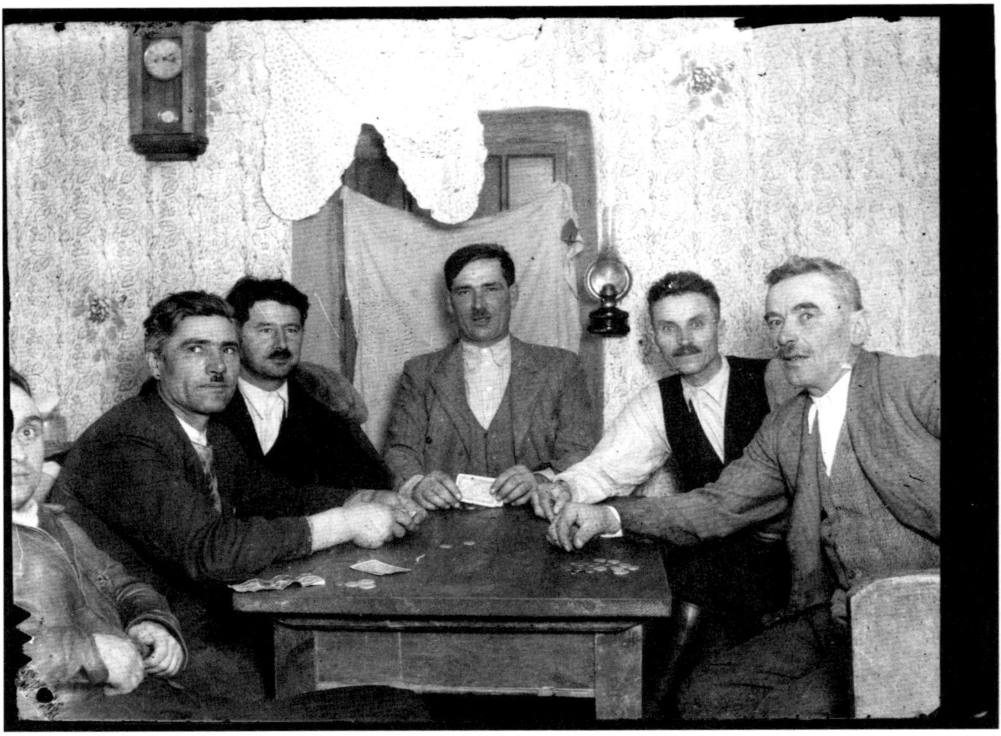

84

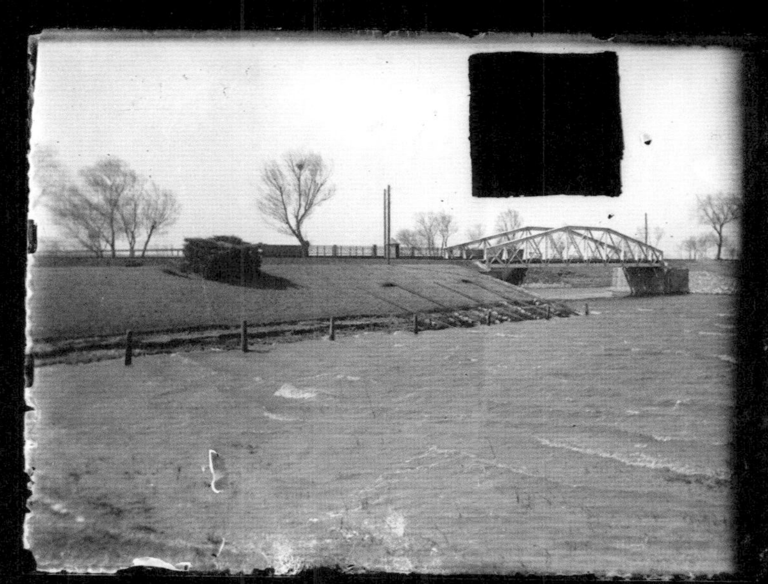

84

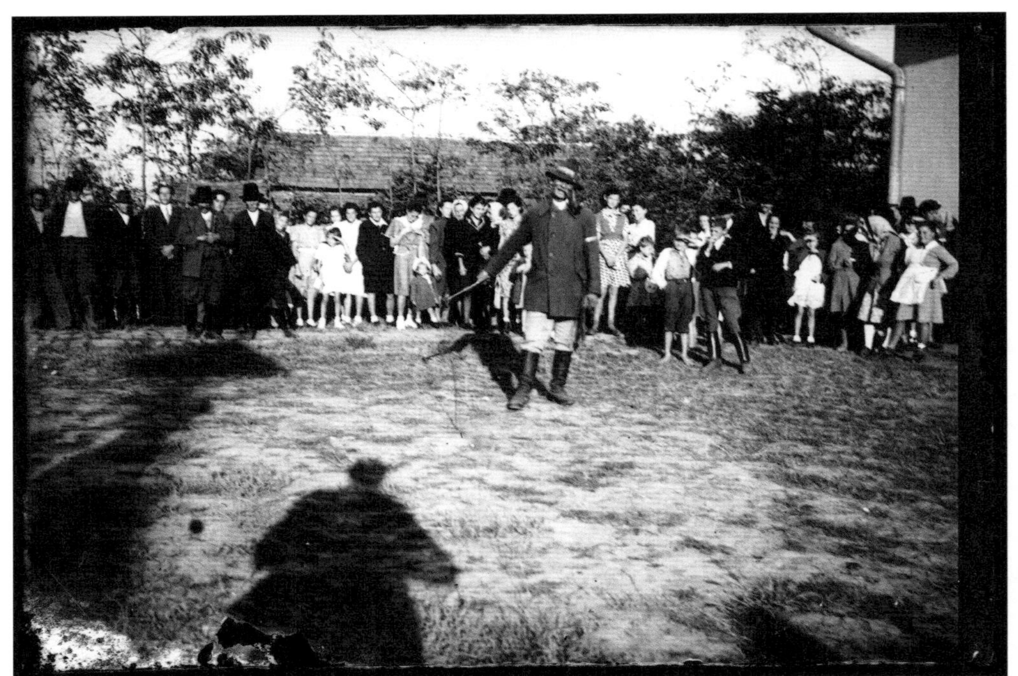

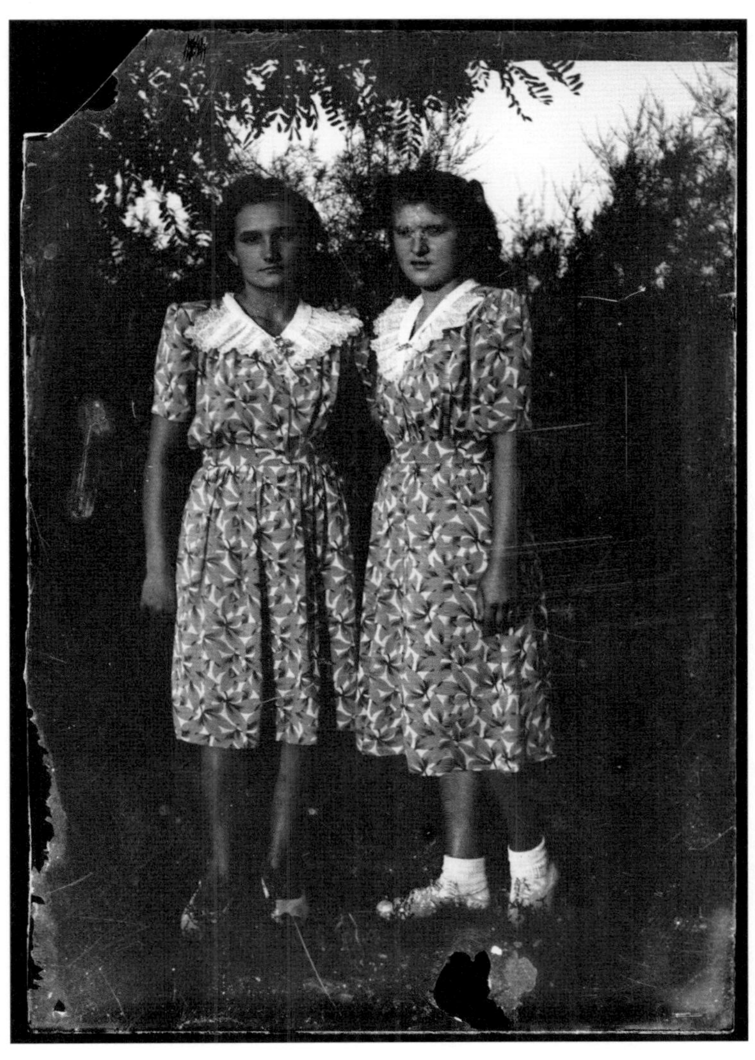

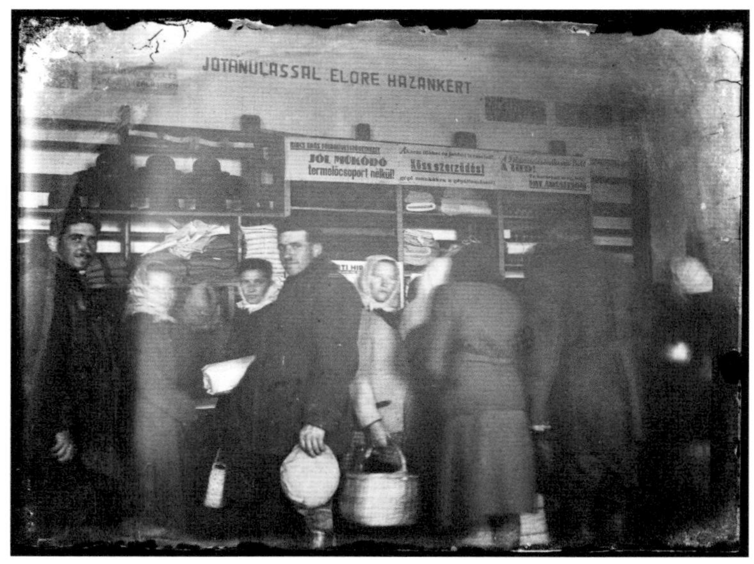

JÓTANULÁSSAL ELŐRE HAZÁNKÉRT
JÓL MŰKÖDŐ
termelőcsoport nélkül!
Köss szerződést

87

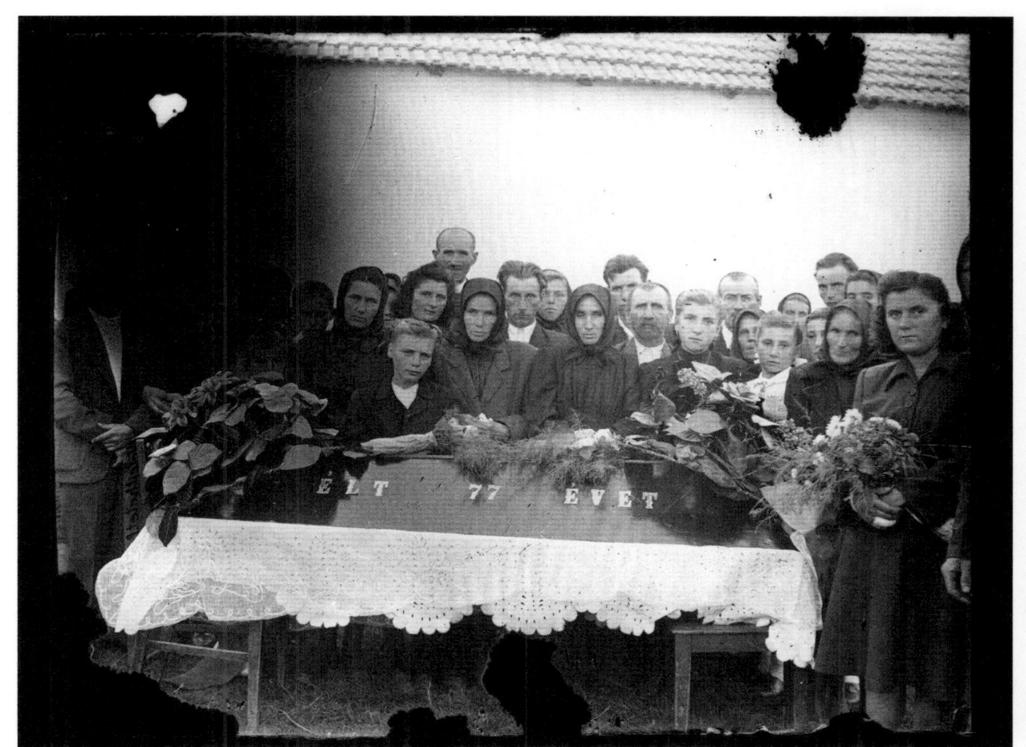
ÉLT 77 ÉVET

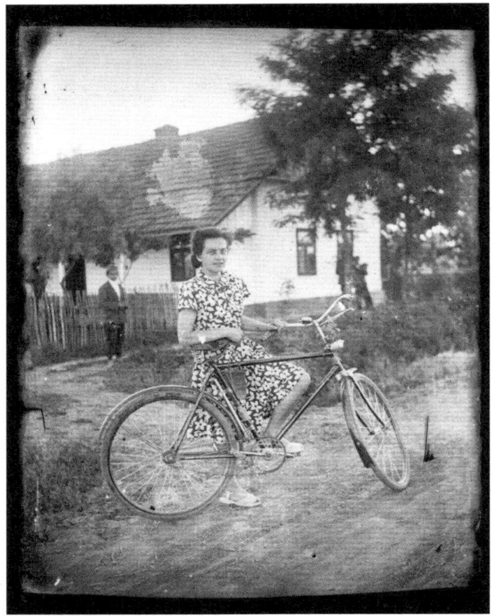

89

90

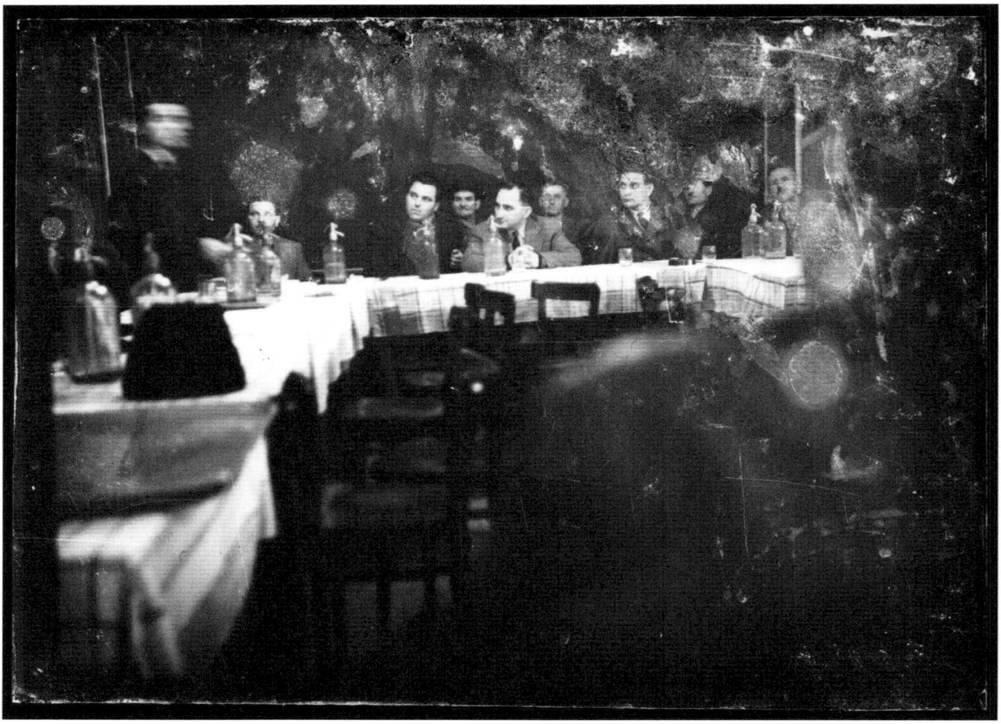

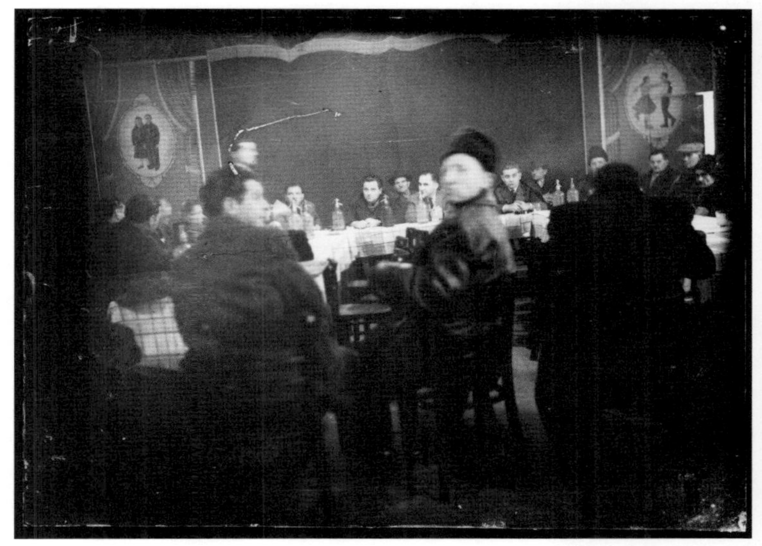

91

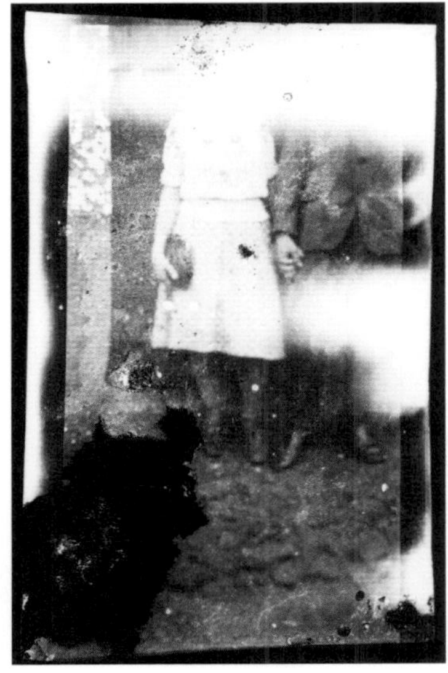

92

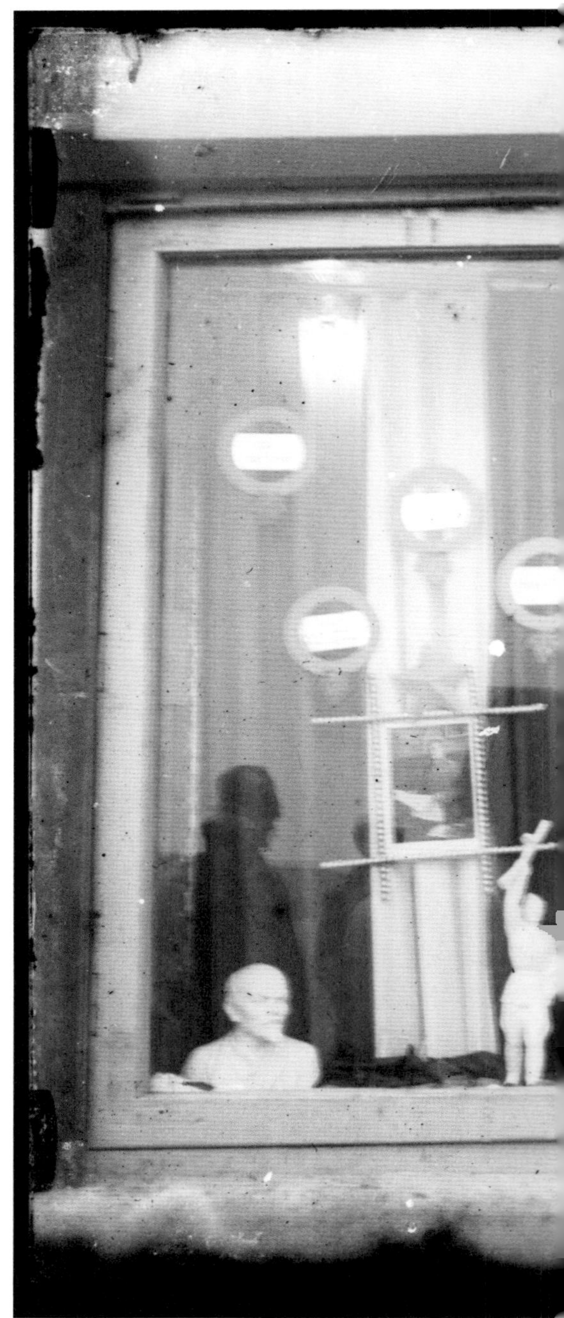

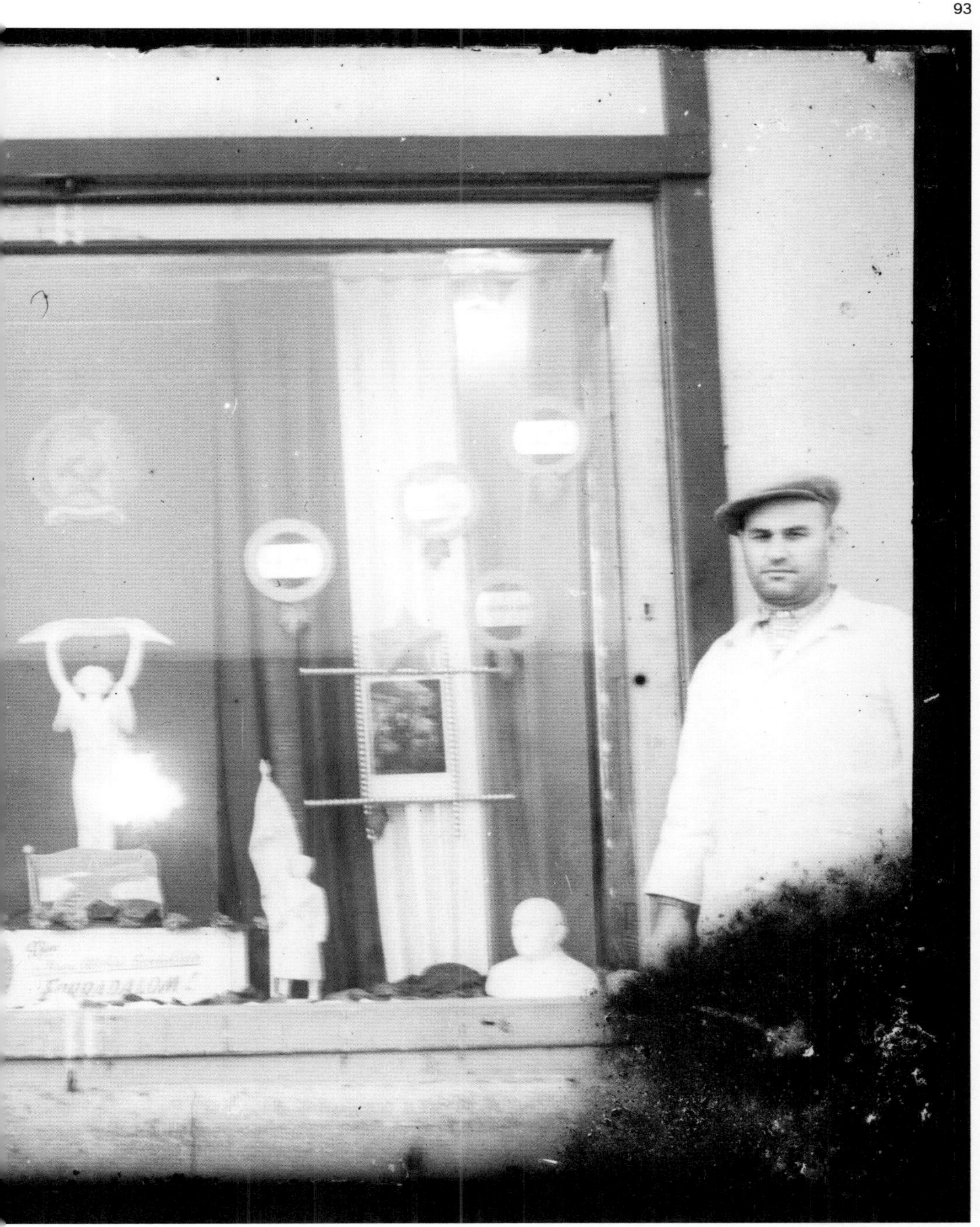

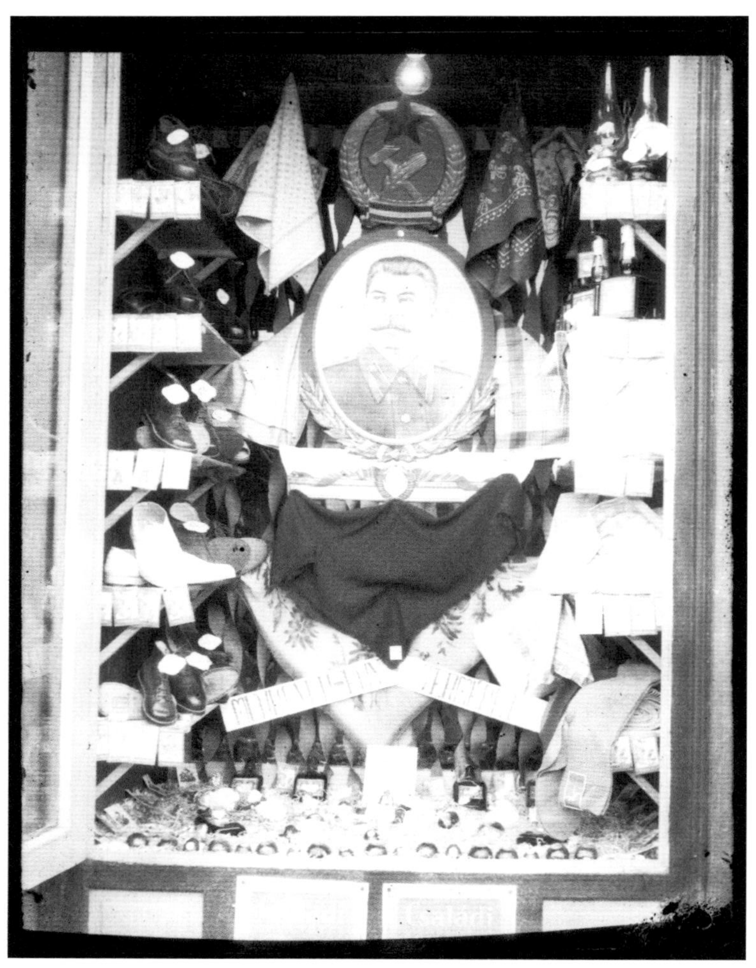

Gergely Papp

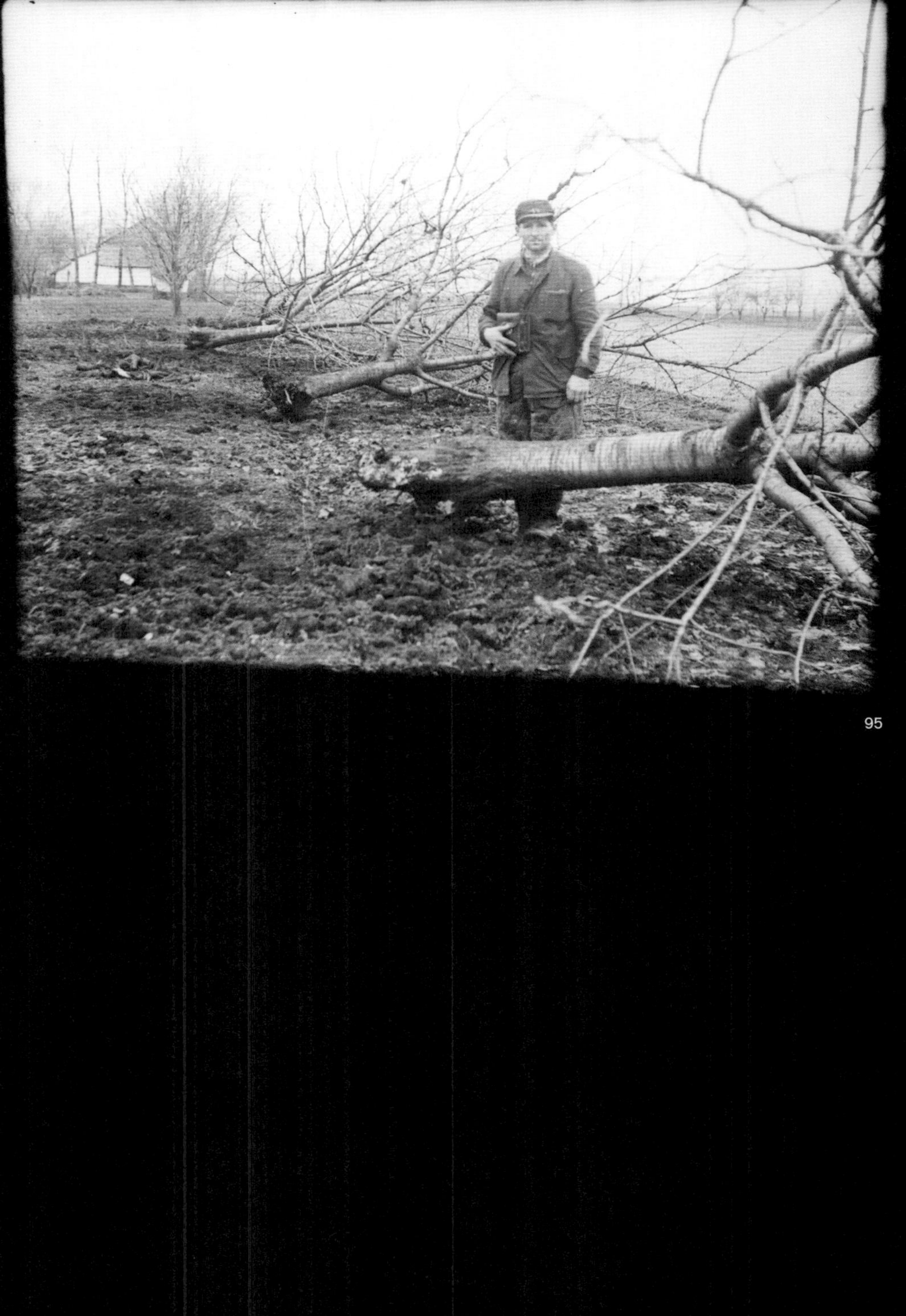

Encountering Gergely Papp

Written by
Tibor Miltényi

I have been trying to comprehend the Gergely Papp phenomenon for over twenty years. As a man, he was as large as life and as enchanting as his photos, which, independently of him, turned out so magically. His charismatic and dignified personality, which stood completely outside of reality and time, enthralled me whenever I met him. Back then, over two decades ago, he was living in terrifying isolation at the edge of his village. It was hard talking to him, because everything reminded him of his world-redeeming idées fixes. He kept repeating these, varying the elements as and when he felt like it. These compulsive statements of his did not get boring with time because the stories would always come as they occurred to him, linking to one another through the flow alone; he would always say the same things, but in a completely different way, in the very same way as his pictures.

At first, I was distinctly annoyed that he did not want to remember his photography, and it seemed to irritate him that I persistently asked about it. In actual fact, there was not that much he could say about his photos, since his photographs were outside the constellation of his delusional worldview. The only reason he had not thrown the negatives away was because he had never thrown anything away in his life—the physical memories of seventy-five years were heaped up in a ghostly pile in his dark room.

Gergely Papp was born in Pusztaecseg (now Ecsegfalva) in Eastern Hungary on the 16th of October 1922 into a poor peasant family with three boys and a girl. In 1928, his parents built the farmstead on the outskirts of the village where he would live for the rest of his life. From the age of four, he assisted around the farm, herding pigs. He did not complete his elementary education and could barely read, write, and count. Dyslexia was an unknown concept at the time in Pusztaecseg and children with such learning difficulties were not given any special attention in school. He never read a book in his life and was completely devoid of intellectual curiosity. "I hate books," he said when I met him in 1997. He was quite proud of his infantilism. At the same time, he was wonderfully practical, and was particularly good at mechanical repairs. He had also taught himself to play music well; he would often perform until dawn for the locals in the village tavern on his clarinet.

His brother István, too weak to take on his share of the heavy physical labour of peasant life, went off to be a photographer's apprentice in the nearby town. He taught his teenage brother to take pictures in the photographer's studio in Kisújszállás in 1938. Gergely had an instinctive attraction to anything mechanical, and immediately took to photography. He never devoted himself to farming and animal husbandry, preferring to play music and cards in the tavern and take pictures. While István only produced formal studio portraits, Gergely was interested in anything that counted as an event in village life: christenings, harvests, First Communion, hunting, weddings, funerals, and so on. But he also took great pleasure in immortalizing the simple everyday things, as well as his desire to document the entire population of the village. As to what subject matter was most important to him, we have the evidence of an early nighttime self portrait from around 1940, taken with a self-timer [PG 13—01]. In the middle of this image is a motorbike that he is disassembling, his clarinet on the ground with his tools, while in the background is a throng of villagers gaping at these little wonders.

His goal was merely to make gifts of his printed photographs to the people they recorded. This friendly gesture was an attempt to earn their respect. Since he preferred to drink, play cards and music, ride his motorcycle and take photographs instead of the more traditional tasks of peasant labour—living a Bohemian, non-conformist life—he needed the villagers to tolerate this unusual lifestyle. In 1942, his father made a desperate attempt to extricate his son from among his drinking companions in the tavern. They moved to Budapest, just the two of them, for a few months, to work in a factory. This was when he took his only extant street view of Budapest, and this was where he met the girl he wanted to marry, though he never did.

In October 1943, Gergely was called up and became the regimental photographer for the Sárospatak Barracks. His brother István ended up as an aerial photographer in Budapest. From a military perspective, Germany and her allies had already lost the Second World War, but there was a long way to go before surrender. During his time as a soldier, he took group shots and portraits, but he also continued to photograph his surroundings. In September 1944, he was wounded seriously during a military exercise, and was treated in hospital with several of his companions. This was where he took an especially bizarre picture, which he decided to call *A Woman in the Barracks* (1944), discussed later in this essay. In 1945, after he was captured by the Soviets near Kassa, he was taken to Samara, where he worked on the hydroelectric dam. Weighing a mere 28 kilograms, he was not permitted to return home until August. István only returned in 1949, while Jóska, the youngest, being a child soldier, had already been released in the summer of 1945; he, however, was haunted for the rest of his life by the horrors he had witnessed and suffered from a severe psychosis.

After his recovery, Gergely returned to his former life before his enlistment, unwilling to learn a trade, and preferring to carry on taking photos, playing cards, drinking, and making music in the tavern. His philosophy was "Let the People Work!" 1948 saw the beginnings of Soviet-style Communist dictatorship in Hungary. In 1950, the land was nationalized, the peasants forced onto collective farms. Papp, like others, was shocked by this inexorable state terror; the only thing they had been left with was their house. In his thinking, this was the dawn of a new era. Everything before 1950 was "before", and everything after that date was "now." He had never been a fan of agricultural labour, but now he had some justification in saying that he would not work until they gave him back his land. In 1951, he and his brother were working in a photographic lab in Budapest, but, since they did not join the Communist Party, they were dismissed. Papp then became a set decorator for a provincial travelling circus, but by the mid-50s, he had moved back to the farm with his parents and would never leave it again.

The 1956 Revolution and the struggle for independence was mostly centered on Budapest, with Soviet troops brutally repressing it.

The only significant impact of the Revolution in provincial Hungary was that the majority of the collective farms disintegrated and the peasants took back their land. While the Communists had already begun to reaffirm their grip on power by November, it took years for collective farming to be re-established in the countryside. It was only in 1963 that the central state managed to reinstate collective farming throughout the country. This proved a repeat of the trauma of 1950; this time, the state wanted the Papp family's fruit trees. This was the last straw for Gergely Papp. He went out, cut down his trees, and took a final self-portrait in the remains [PG 95—95]. After that point, he entirely stopped taking photographs.

From 1963–1965 he worked as a professional fisherman, but was dismissed because he only came to work when he felt like it. After that, he took up fishing illegally, and was fined for the activity in 1973; he was also often cited by the police for drunk driving. He tried his hand at casual jobs: he collected snails and leeches, set traps for gophers, and raised pheasants. In 1965, his elderly parents moved from the farm to the nearby town of Berettyóújfalu, to be with their youngest child, Irma, who was a head nurse at the local hospital. Gergely's father died in 1967 and his mother in 1970. From 1965 on, there were only two people left on the farm, Gergely and his brother Jóska— who continued to suffer from psychosis. Irma eventually got Jóska transferred into her care where he spent the rest of his life. István had opened his own photographic studio in Simontornya in the 1950s. He got married, but the marriage was not a success. As a pensioner, he bought a house in Ecsegfalva in 1981. He would have liked Gergely to move in with him, but the latter would not hear of it. István died in 1987, and from 1981 Gergely lived in total isolation on the decrepit farm until his death at the end of February 2000.

Gergely Papp was completely untrained when it came to art: he took the word to mean acting. The only photographs he had seen were the ones in a village photographer's shop. He made pictures that were purely descriptive and functional, without any artistic intent. Despite this indifferent attitude, almost half of the roughly 300 negatives I have seen had outstanding aesthetic merit. His paranoid personality may help us get closer to the key to the Gergely Papp phenomenon. Paranoia, in itself, is a gentle form of psychosis, somewhere between the normal and the pathological. It is normal in that the personality does not collapse: there are no hallucinations and the sufferers are not a danger to themselves or others. At the same time, it is pathological in that the sufferer lives their whole life in the prison of their mistaken beliefs, based on which they create their own compulsive and strange mental state. Gergely was a stubborn obsessive at the mercy of his own bizarre convictions. But photography did not belong in his exalted ideological system. He never thought much of anything about his photographs, considering them just an extension of everyday reality. Consequently, he never understood why things that were farther away looked smaller in his pictures. He always concentrated on the central figure, not the composition of the whole picture. This made for odd excisions, and often his own shadow becoming an unintentional part of the image. He could not understand how a head had been accidentally cut off. He experienced the finished image itself as nothing but the reality of the original situation in which it was taken. He was also unable to understand how an image could be important to someone who was not in it.

If Gergely's paranoia influenced his approach, his dyslexia might give us insights into the character of his images. The symptoms of dyslexia include, among other things, excessive attention to insignificant details, reversing left and right, and difficulties with memory and time. These are sometimes clearly identifiable in his images, in the way that details that have otherwise nothing in common are gathered together, the shifting of the main figure towards the edges of the frame for no ostensible reason, and their perfect timelessness. He did want to position his subjects in the middle of the frame, or arrange the figures symmetrically and make the horizon horizontal—but he was not always successful. His style, in an aesthetic sense, is not coherent—which is to say he has no style—and yet the images are not chaotic. In the twenty-five years elapsing between 1938 and 1963, the form of his images did not change, and they are characterized persistently by a descriptive naturalism that treated the elements individually. He had no opinions—everything carries the same weight for him—and his compositions are created instinctively, independently of rigor.

Let me make this supposition clearer by examining a few of his more charged images. (The image titles are mine, for ease of identification). In *Infant Enthroned* (1940) [PG 65—63] the task was presumably to produce a simple child portrait of the infant subject. The young Gergely took the task all out of proportion, cobbling together a veritable throne from the chairs and carpets at the farmhouse. This attempt at visual magnificence may seem comical at first, but the result is one of the most severe and at the same time monumental of his creations. Consider the rigid symmetry and the imaginary transcendental plane of the background with its ornamental decoration, the immovable form and the theatrical gesture of the apparently lifeless child—like a figure in a wax museum—who nonetheless seems to know all secrets. The strange aesthetic tendency of this unique, impossible-to-identify style only serves to reinforce the cold, merciless impression. The draperies of the attractive and grandiose installation, with their metallic coldness and layering of planes, also seem to stand outside of time. In this photograph, we are taken from a naive, clumsy, frontally-presented and improvised project into an unknown aesthetic, an almost archaic reality.

Horizons (1942) [PG 24—16] is also a markedly theatrical image, not in the sense of a "posed photo," but rather in the sense that defined anti-realist Mannerism in the sixteenth century, when the formal elements themselves have become the main protagonists of the image thanks to its radical abstraction. Here, the villagers had lined up for a display of gymnastics beside the stream. It's an innocent picture of popular life, which in Papp's interpretation had become an over-articulated abstraction with extreme layering of horizontals and alignment of planes, one behind the other. From a descriptive, natural sight, he manages to make a strange, repetitive, geometric, aesthetic form. The forced and uncanny pulsation of the horizons radiate the presence of another reality alongside real life. This has a strong aesthetic value that makes no statement about its object—attaching no worldly experience of reality—and even does away with style itself.

In *A Woman in the Barracks* (1944) ^(PG 56—52), one sees that behind this vulgar soldier's game lies a real tragedy: in reality, two people died and several more were severely wounded (Papp among them) when a shell exploded during a training exercise. This irreverent photograph was taken in the hospital, the participants being his wounded comrades. This is one of his most intense images, in which every point is a focal point. It is a closed, airless composition that, in the midst of the most intense aesthetic density, not only transforms the obscene irony of the original scene in real life, but also the latter, heavily damaged nature of the negative. Each banal detail glistens in a dark light: the damage seems to erase what was real. The details of bodies on the plane appear to have been frozen in the moment of the earlier, awful explosion. It is impossible to decide just how many figures there are in the picture, since the damaged surfaces present a protruding leg, as well as an ethereal face looking out at us, as if the two dead comrades are also present. There is no frivolity—this is the somber radiance of absoluteness and depth, a frozen flash that lasts forever and is never contemporary.

In *Headstand on the Beach* (1960) ^(PG 18—09), this image is also perfectly turned in on itself, which manages to record the manner of its making. The original idea must have been for the headstand to be captured in the middle of the image, in front of a level horizon. The protagonist, however, has slipped and the horizon is skewed, though we can see from the accidental shadow that Papp used a tripod, having arranged everything carefully in advance. His huge shadow self-portrait, through which he is both present and not, as well as the figure on its head, complete each other like positive and negative units. This is a masterful

symmetry, imbued with meaning, and it even speaks richly in the dead space of the background. It is an image that is enchantingly fragmented and in which there is no artistic posturing, only the hypnotic radiance of timeless monumentality. Even the moment is posed, even the reality of daily life is abstracted, even the ironic is serious, even errors are transcendent as well as all the details, each as important as the other, in this unusual aesthetic environment.

With *Me and the Bridge* (1963) ^(PG 85—84) Papp was fascinated with the small, steel bridge at the edge of Ecsegfalva all his life. He considered it a miracle of engineering. It was this overwhelming passion for the bridge that he was trying to express with this unlikely "ur-selfie," with its terrifying finality. He scratched out a square on the negative above the bridge, to insert his own portrait. Although the portrait was never added, the black square was nonetheless there. The result is an image with an abysmally cold tone and somber, ethereal majesty. The square exists neither in the image nor in the viewer's field of vision, but in an independent space. This is not a case of the "picture within the picture" that persists in the history of art, but the unknown case of an image invading an image from outside. Because of the powerful aura of transcendental presence, the image is pierced and collapses in on itself. Essential form, as a substantive feature of art, is also the revelation of pure geometry. The square is one of the most spiritual forms; it is a distant yet oppressive force. It is not easy to like, but it has an irresistible flow characteristic of all Papp's memorable photography.

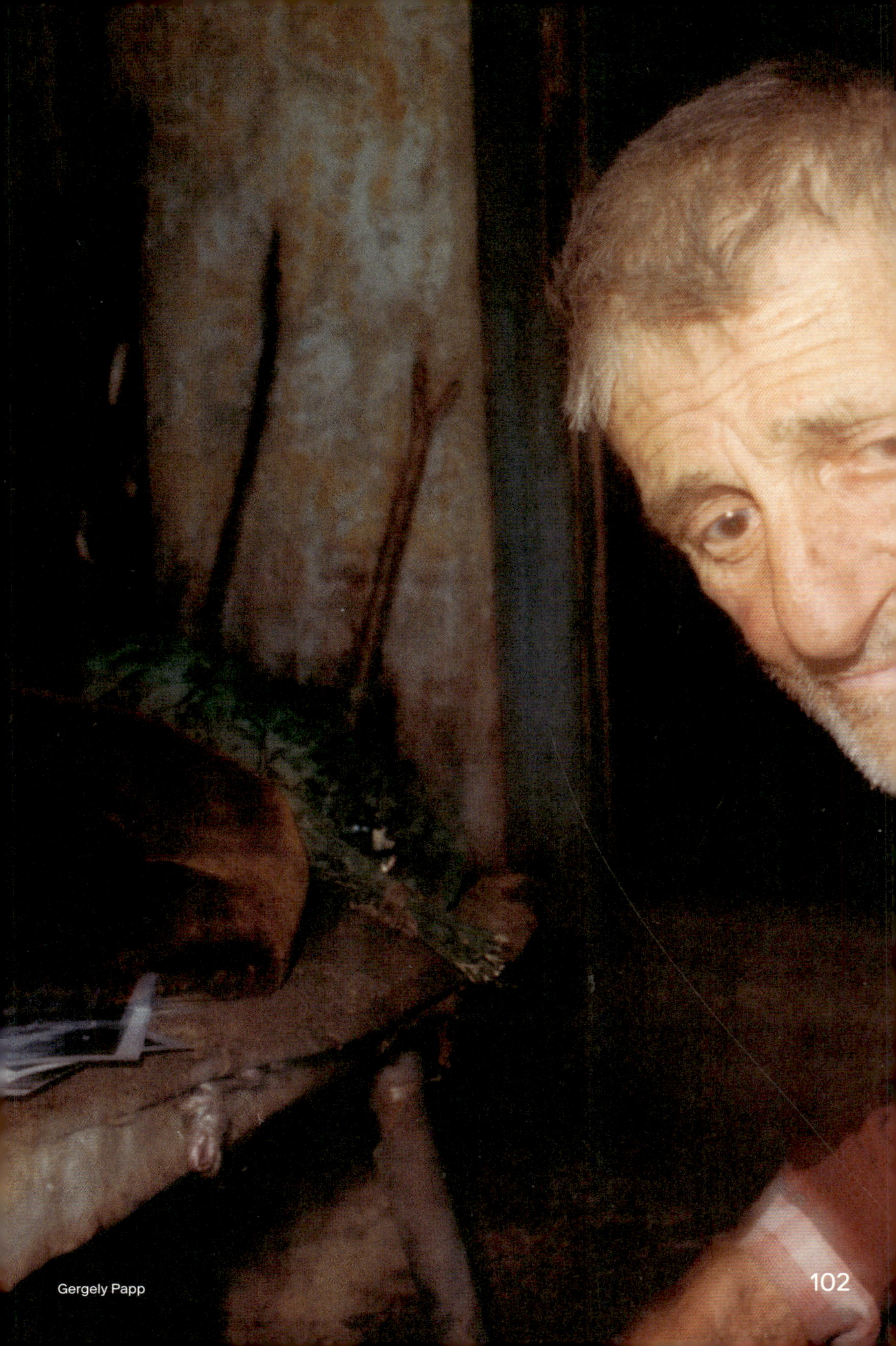

Gergely Papp

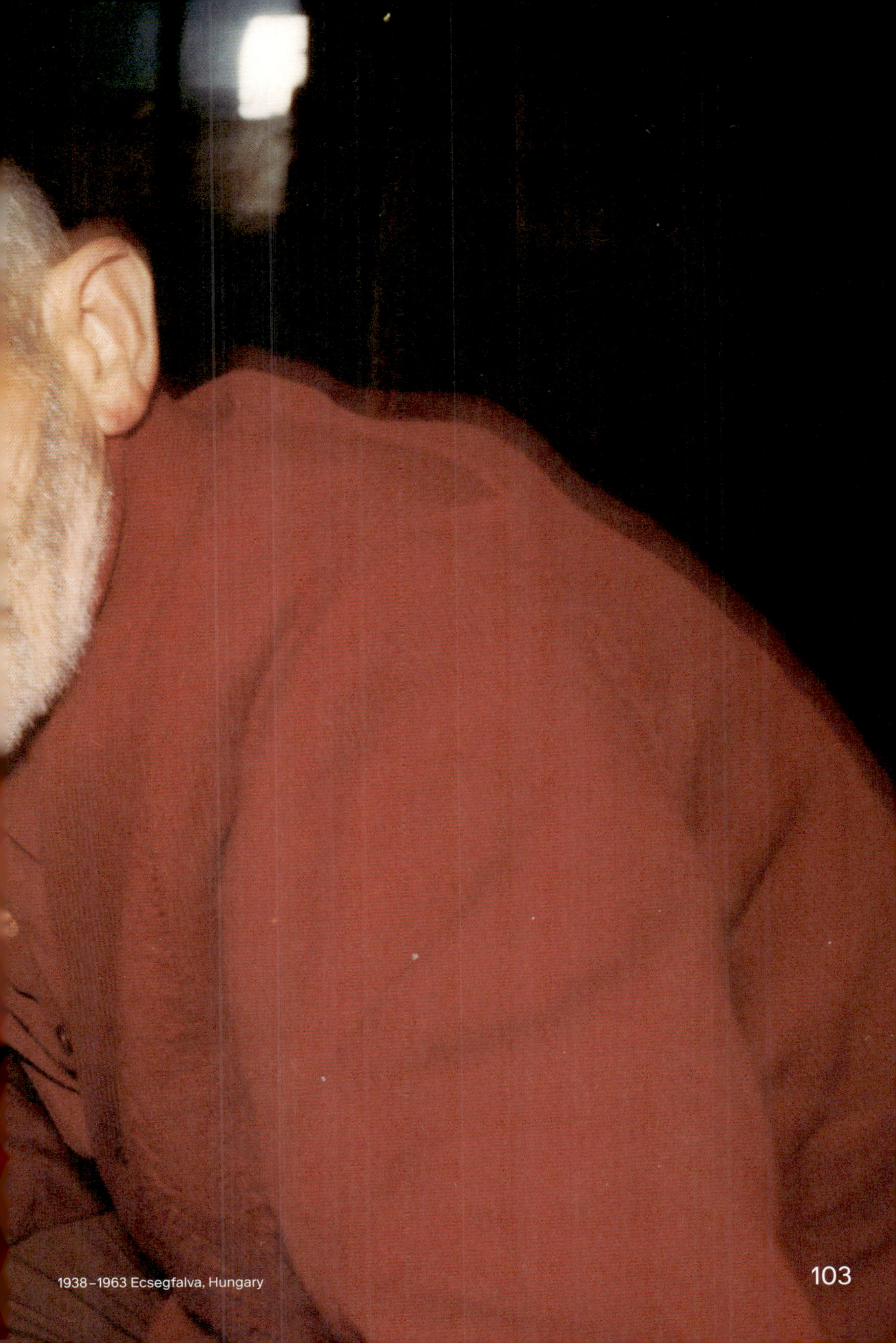

1938–1963 Ecsegfalva, Hungary

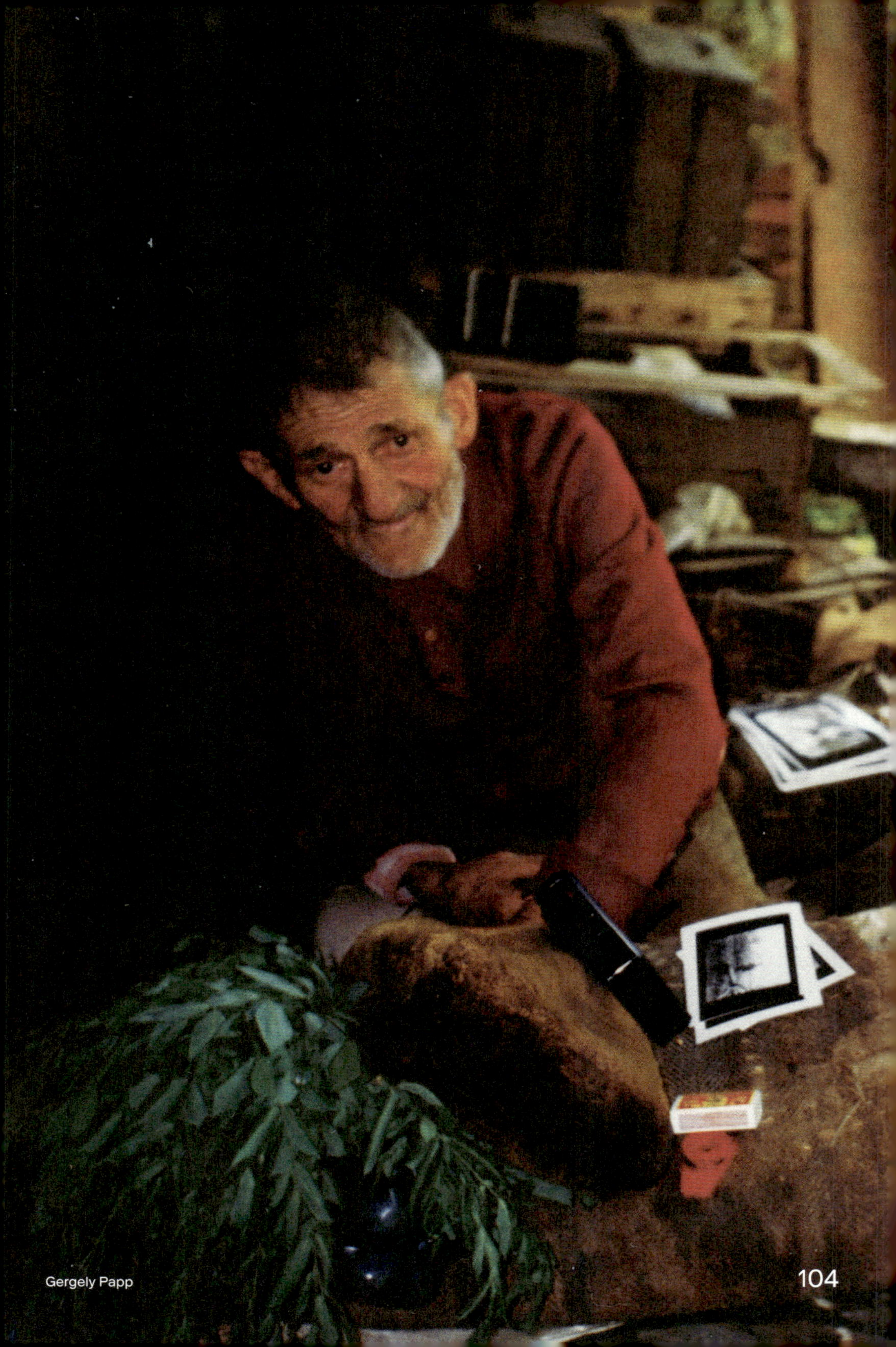

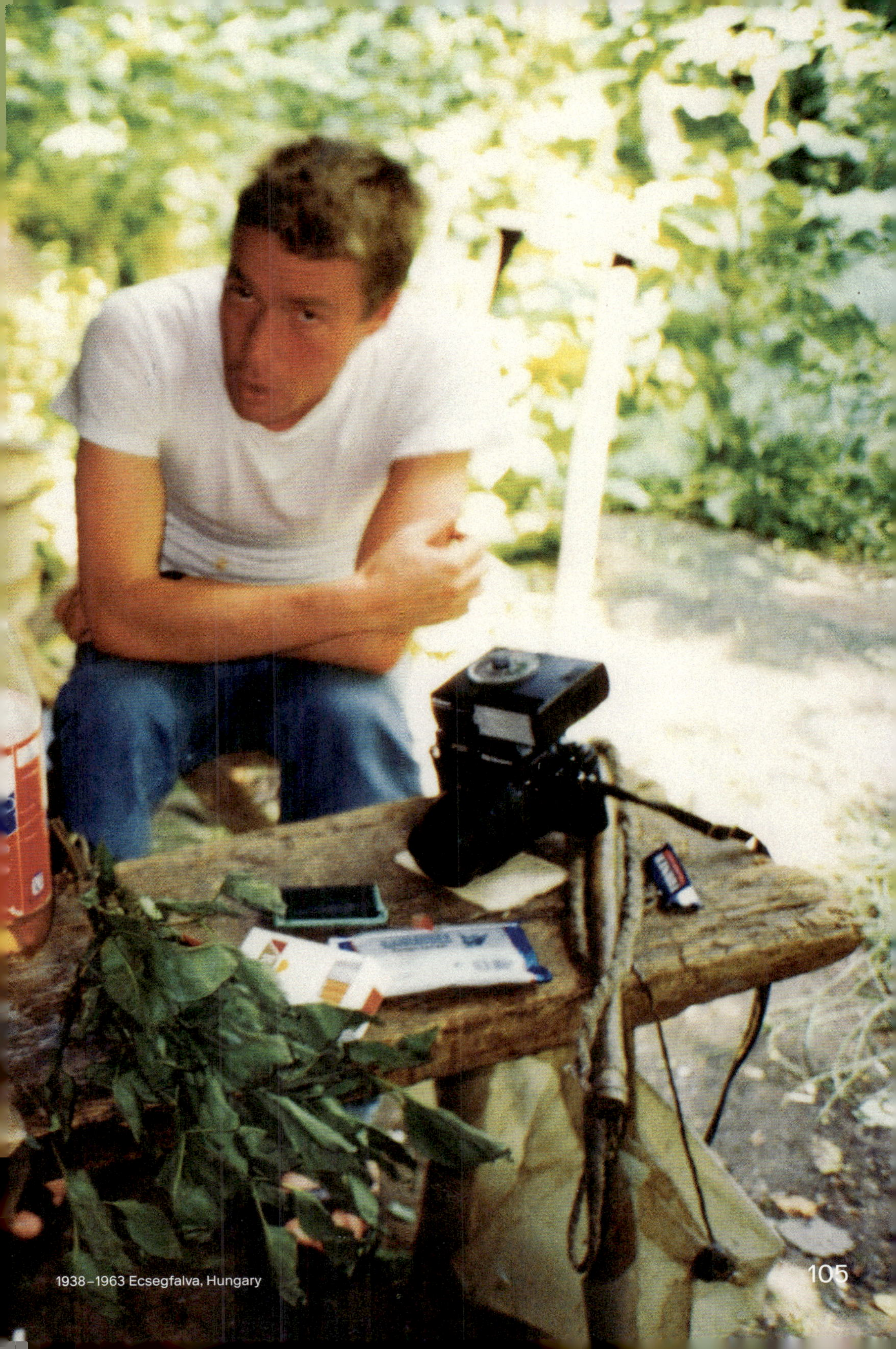

1938–1963 Ecsegfalva, Hungary

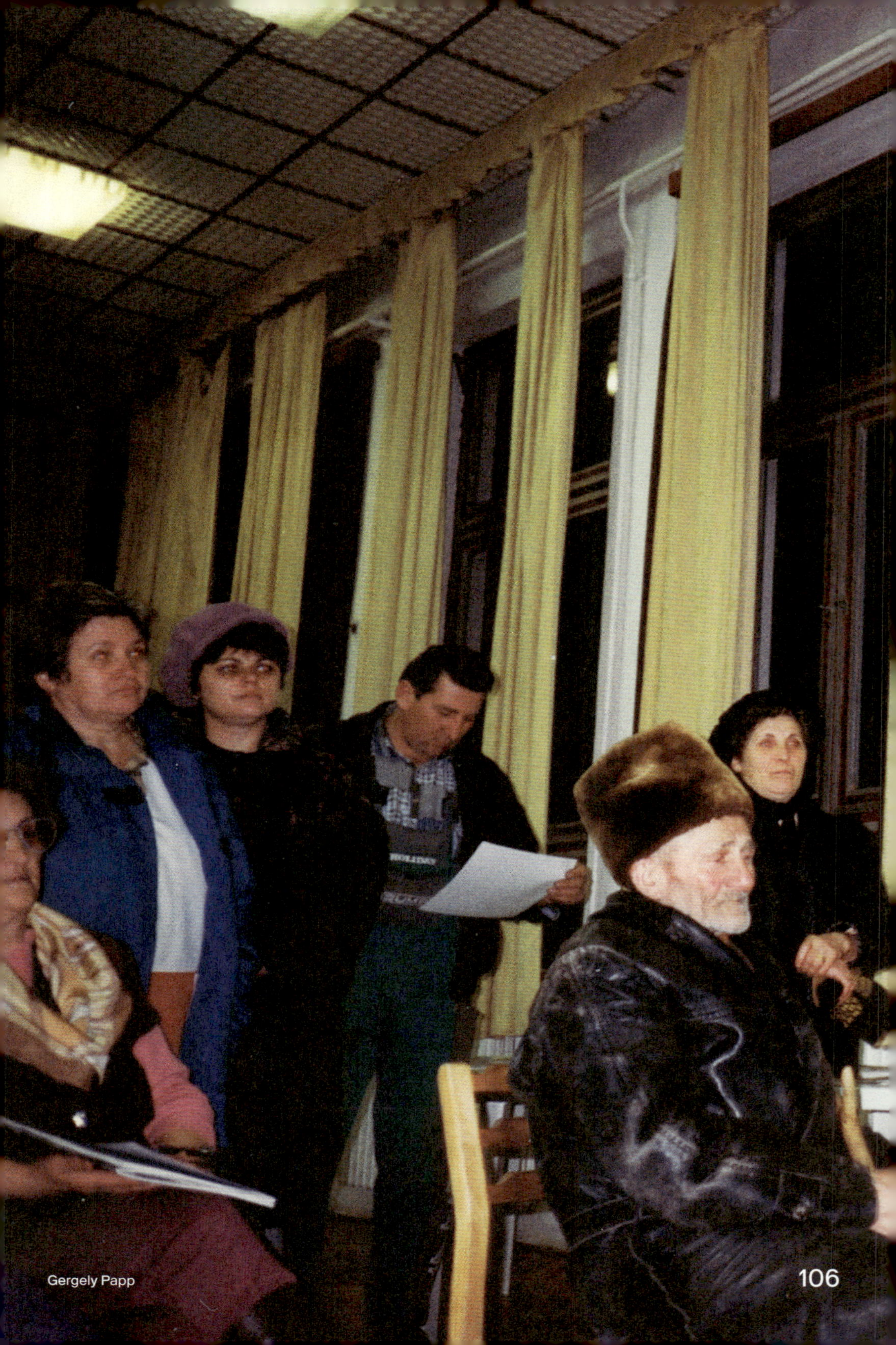

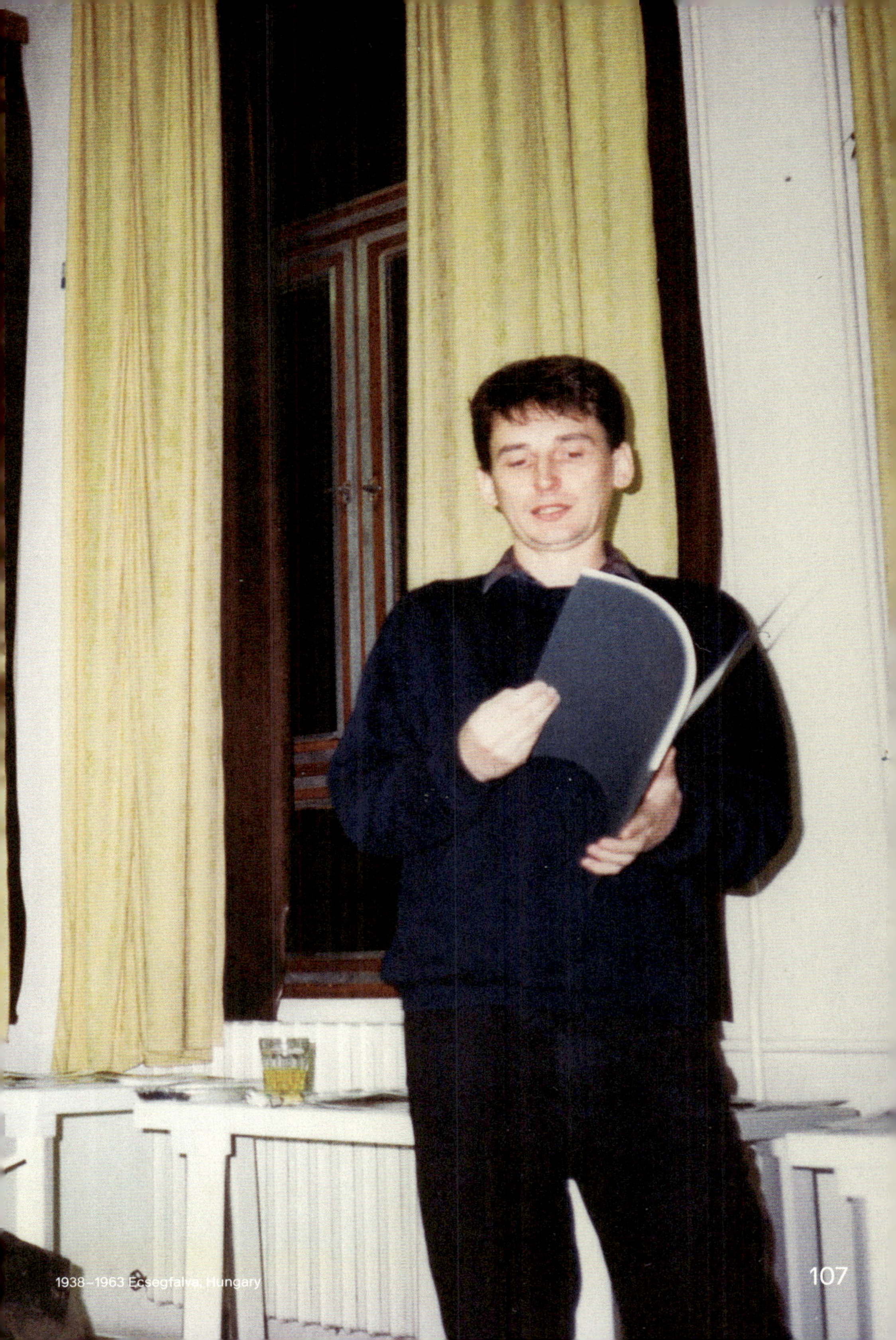

1938–1963 Ecsegfalva, Hungary

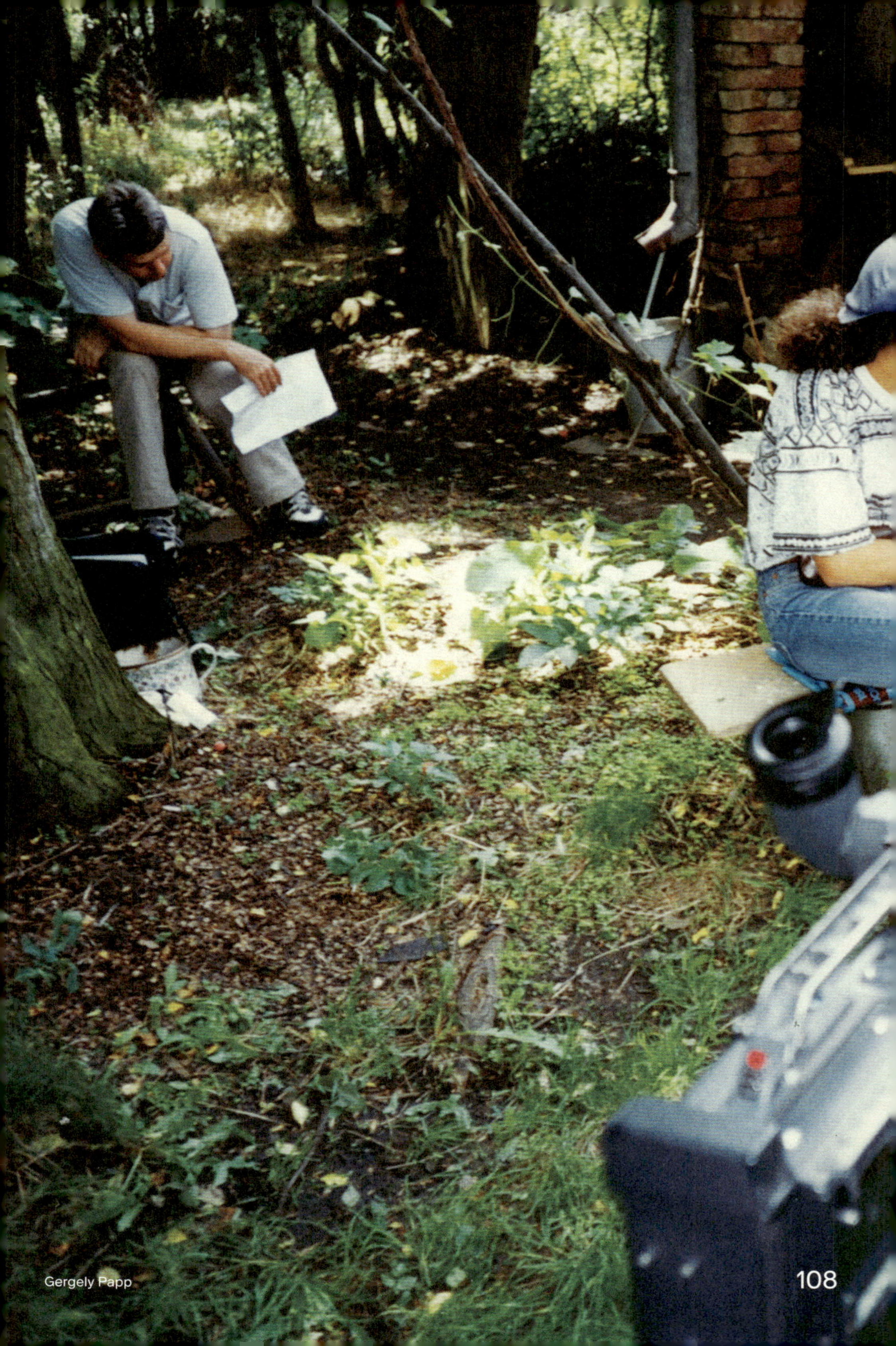

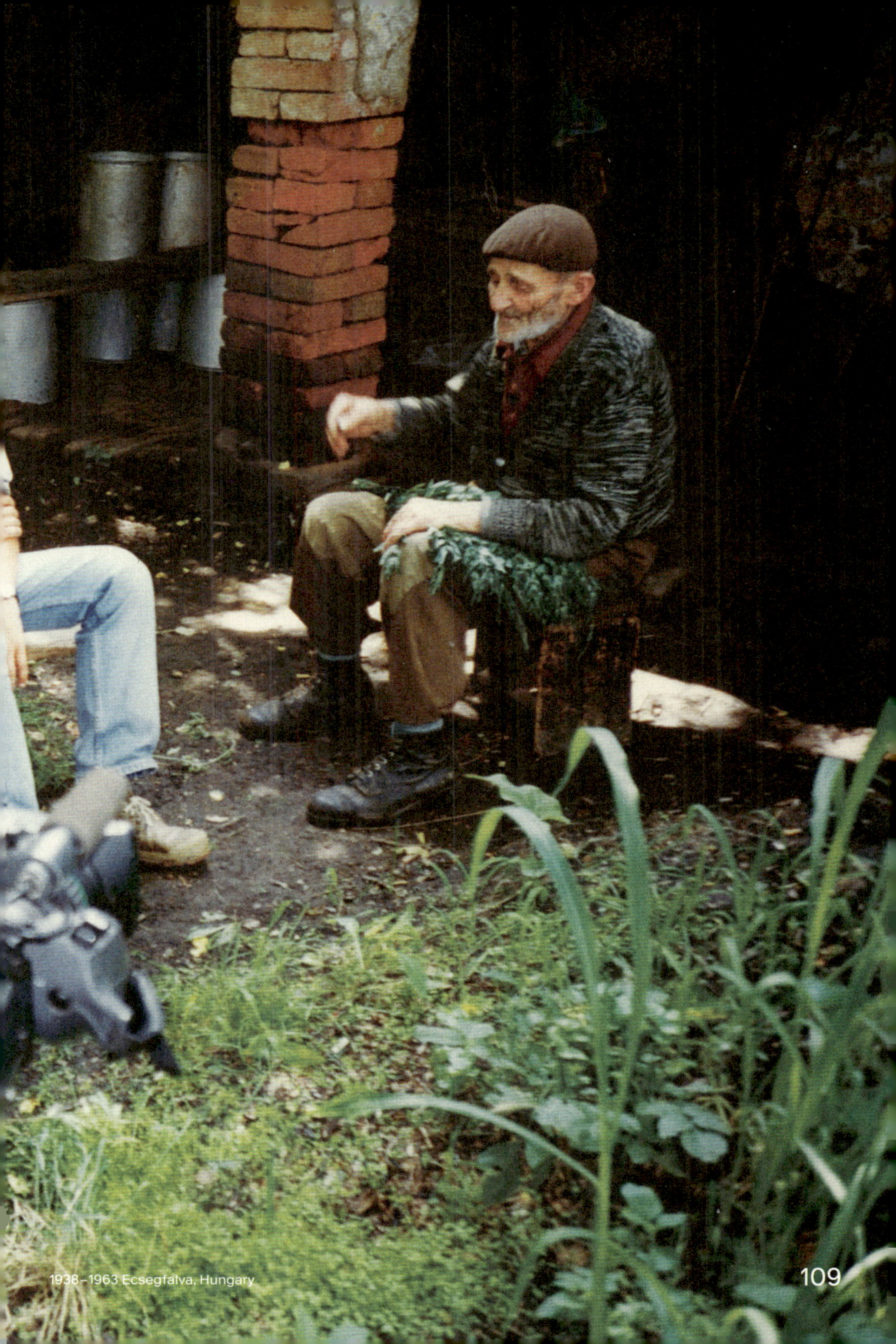

1938–1963 Ecsegfalva, Hungary

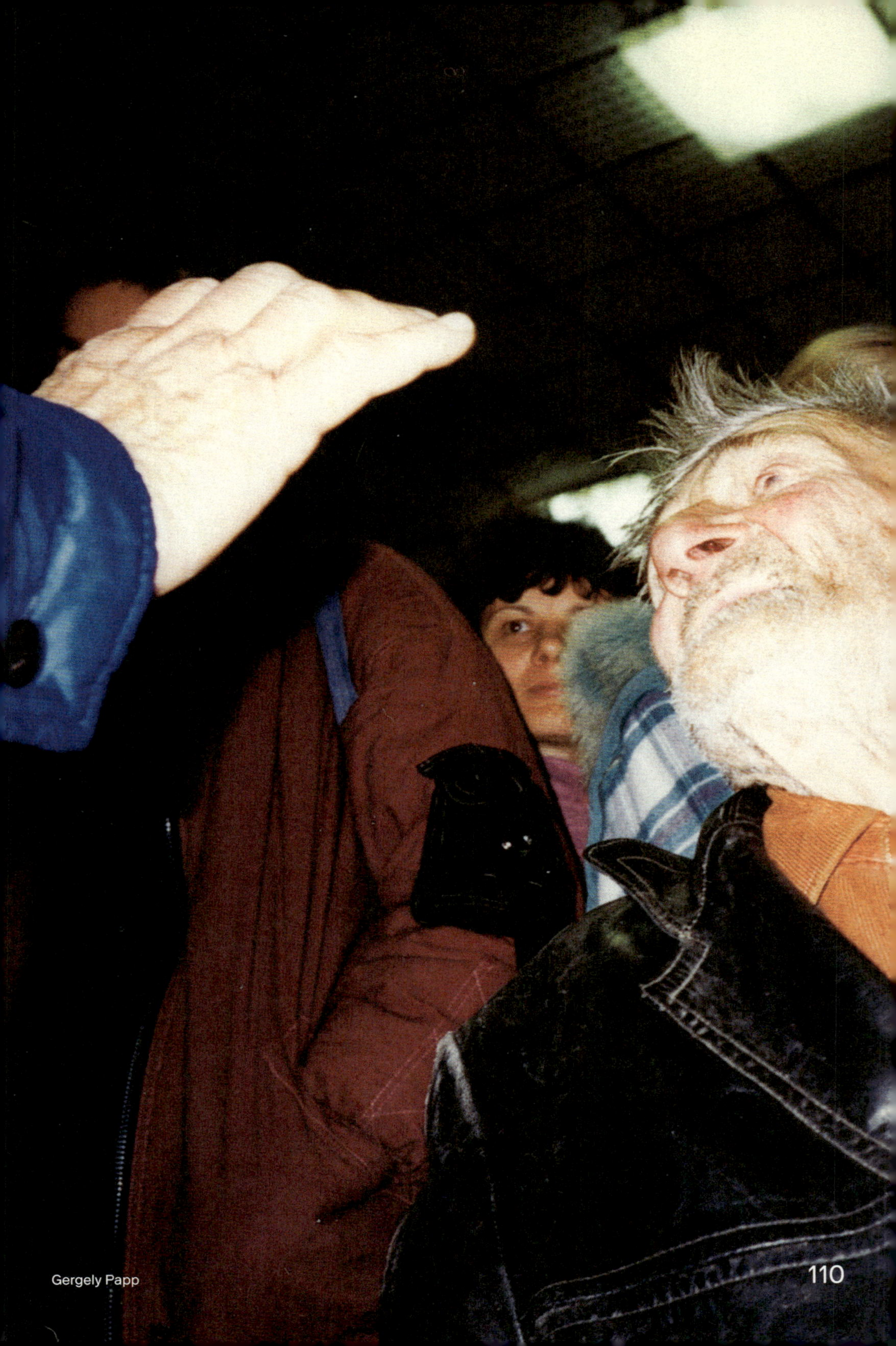

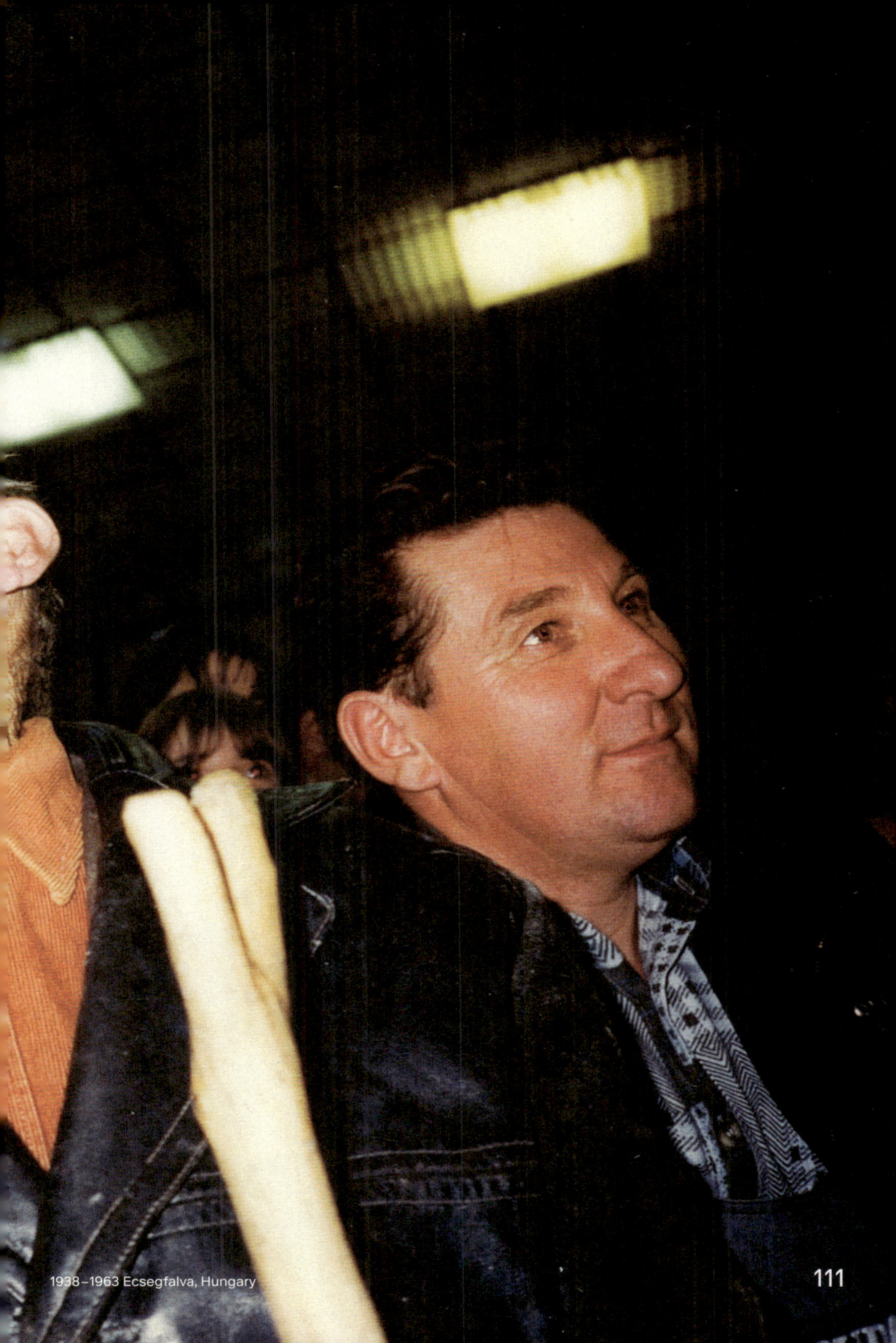

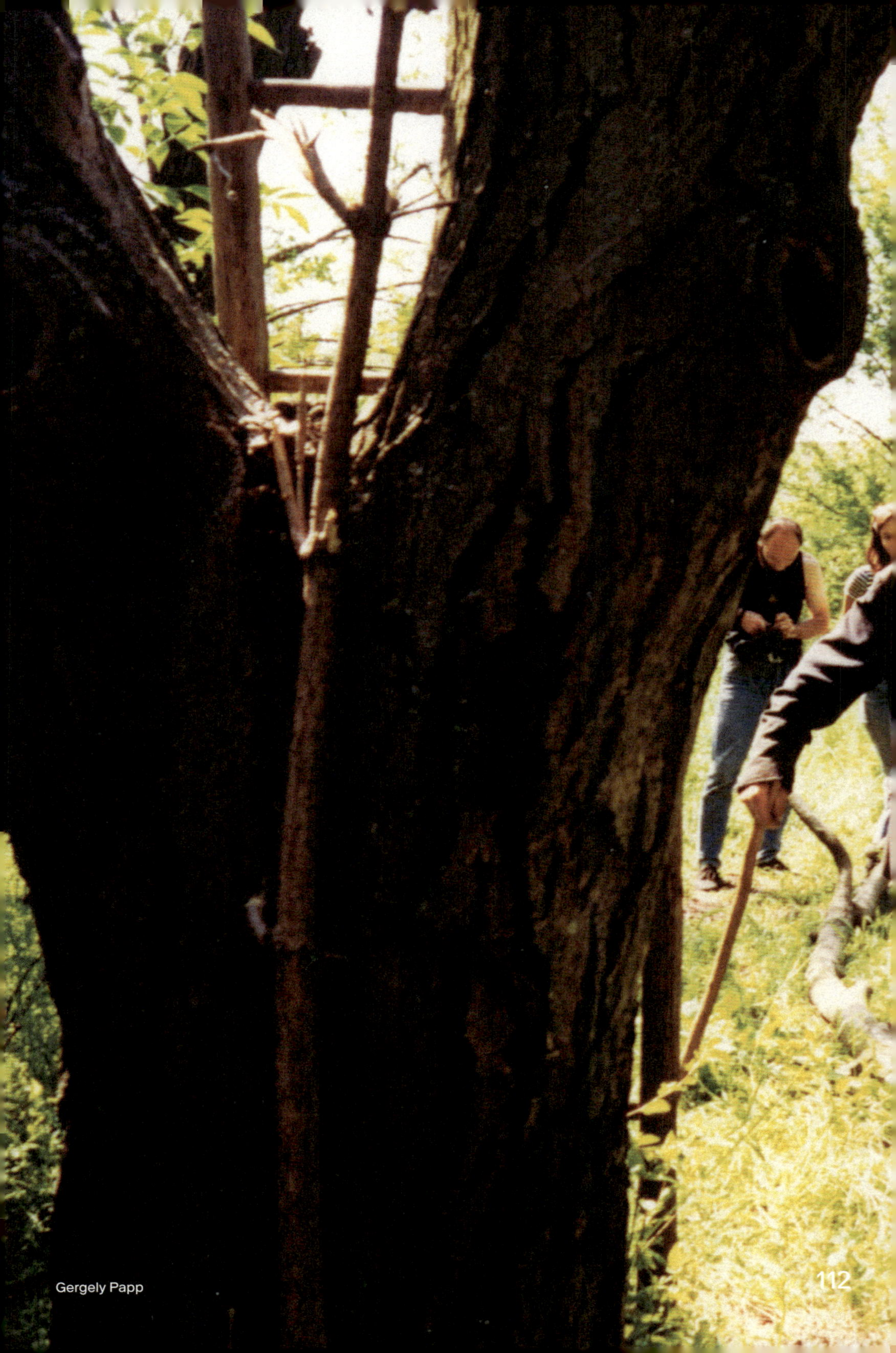

Gergely Papp

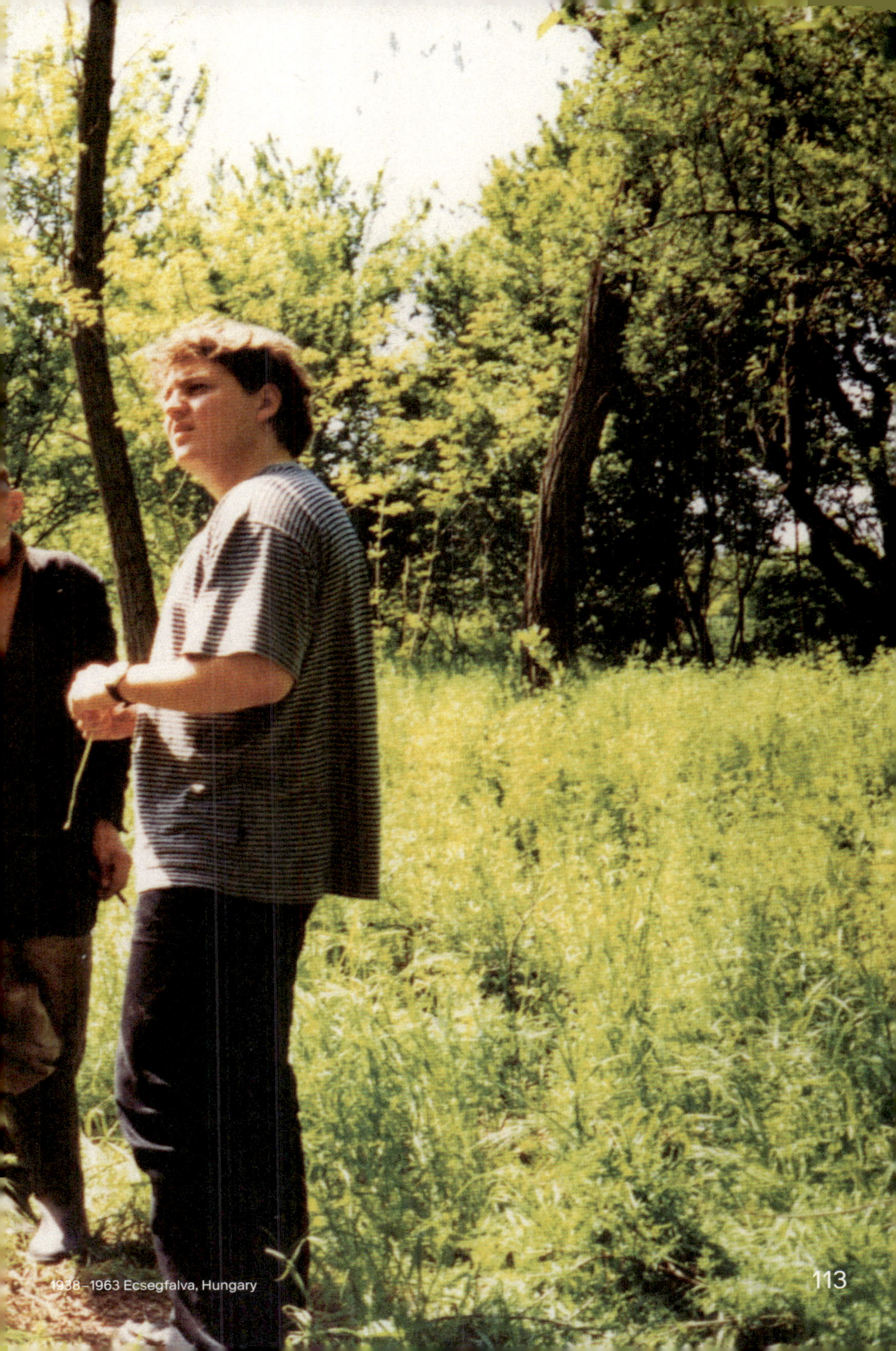

1938–1963 Ecsegfalva, Hungary

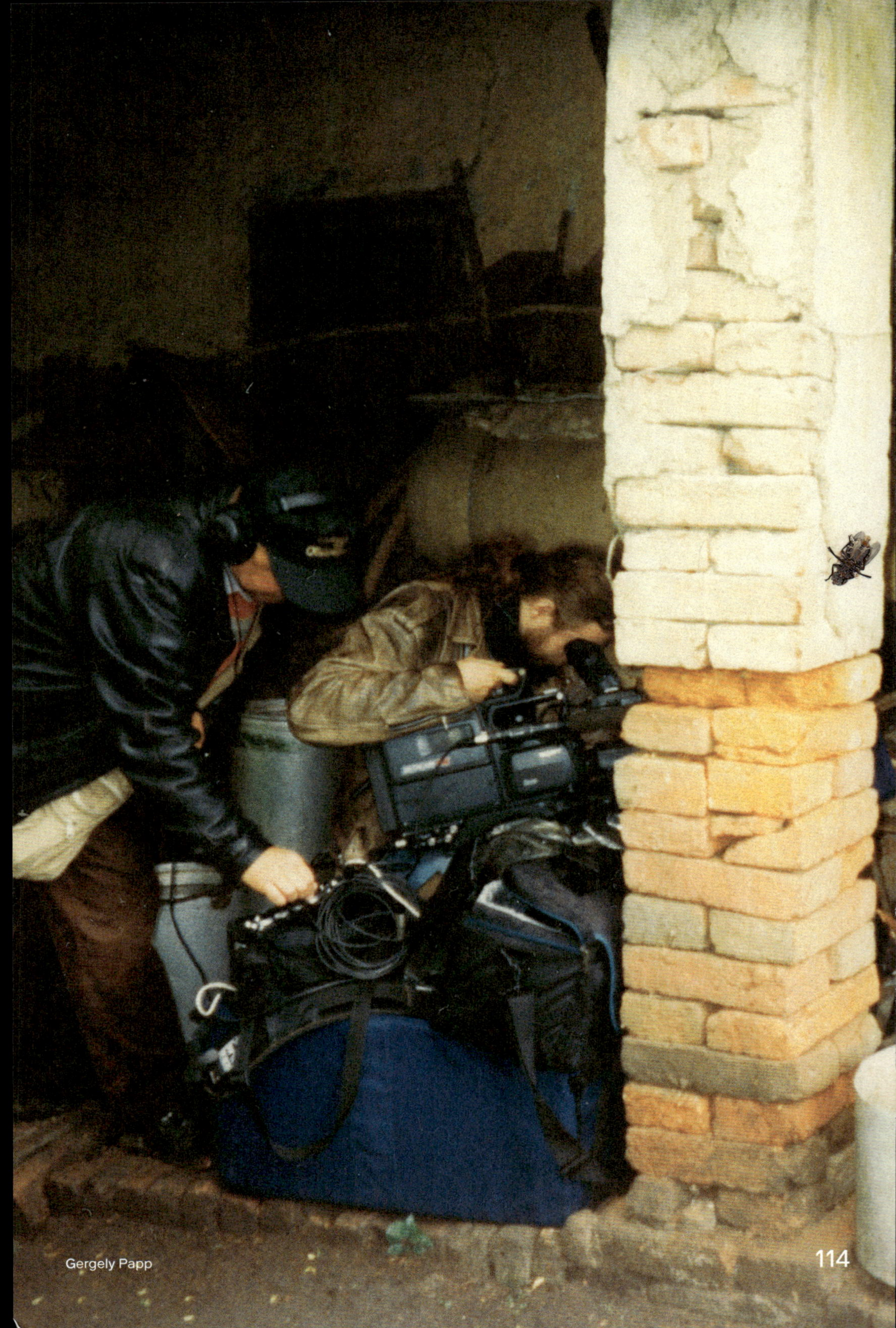

Gergely Papp

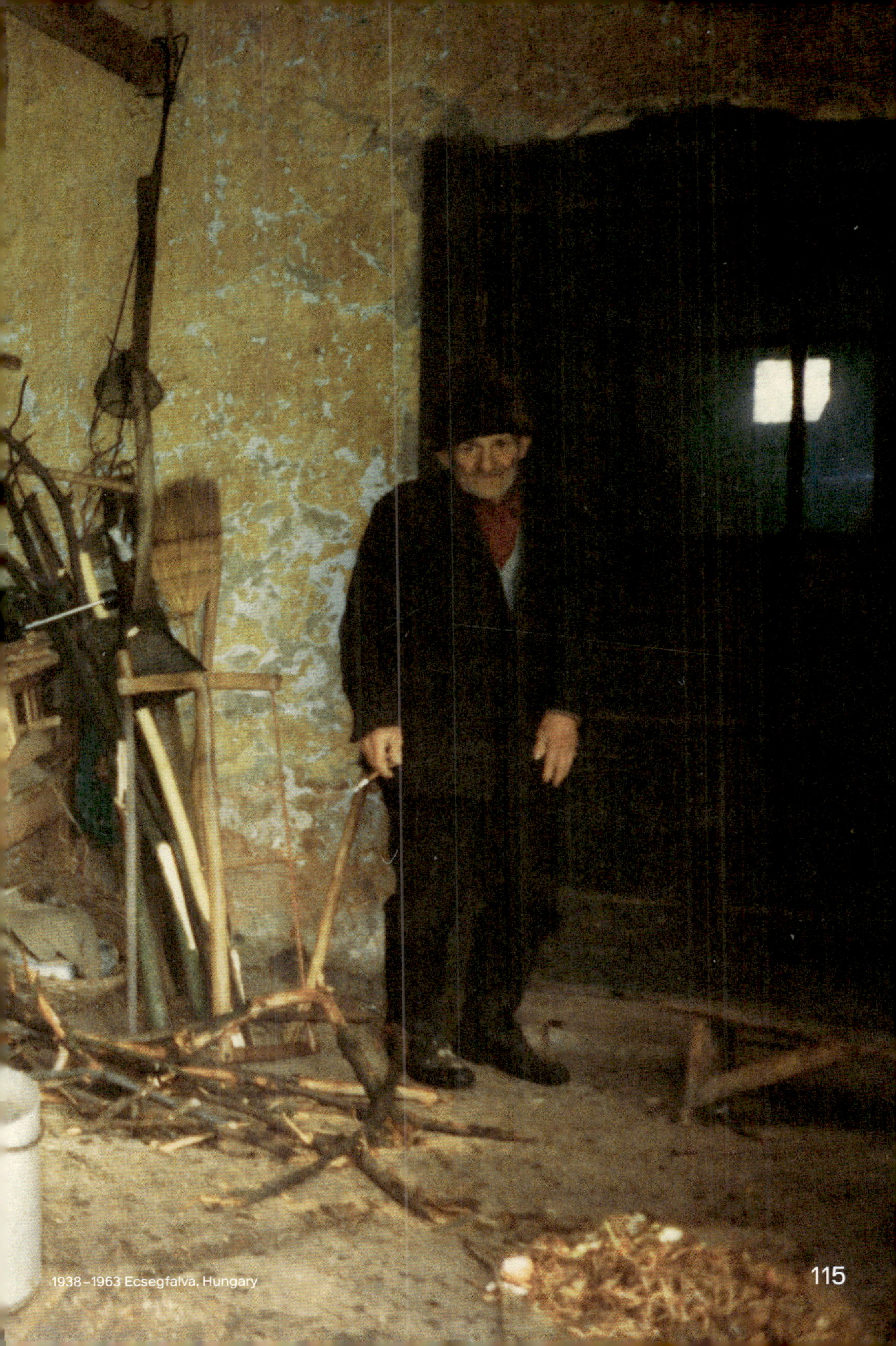

1938–1963 Ecsegfalva, Hungary

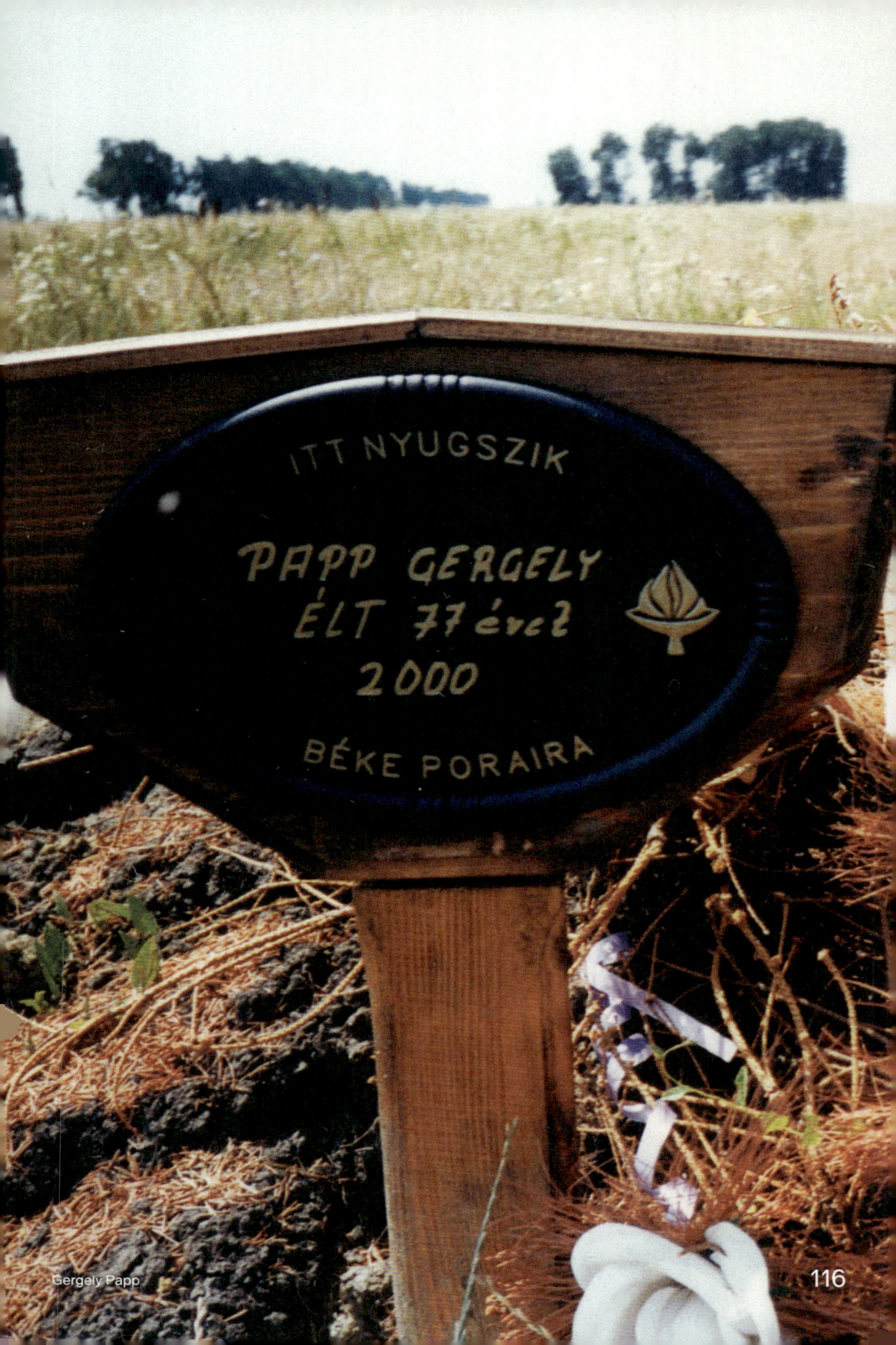

Gergely Papp

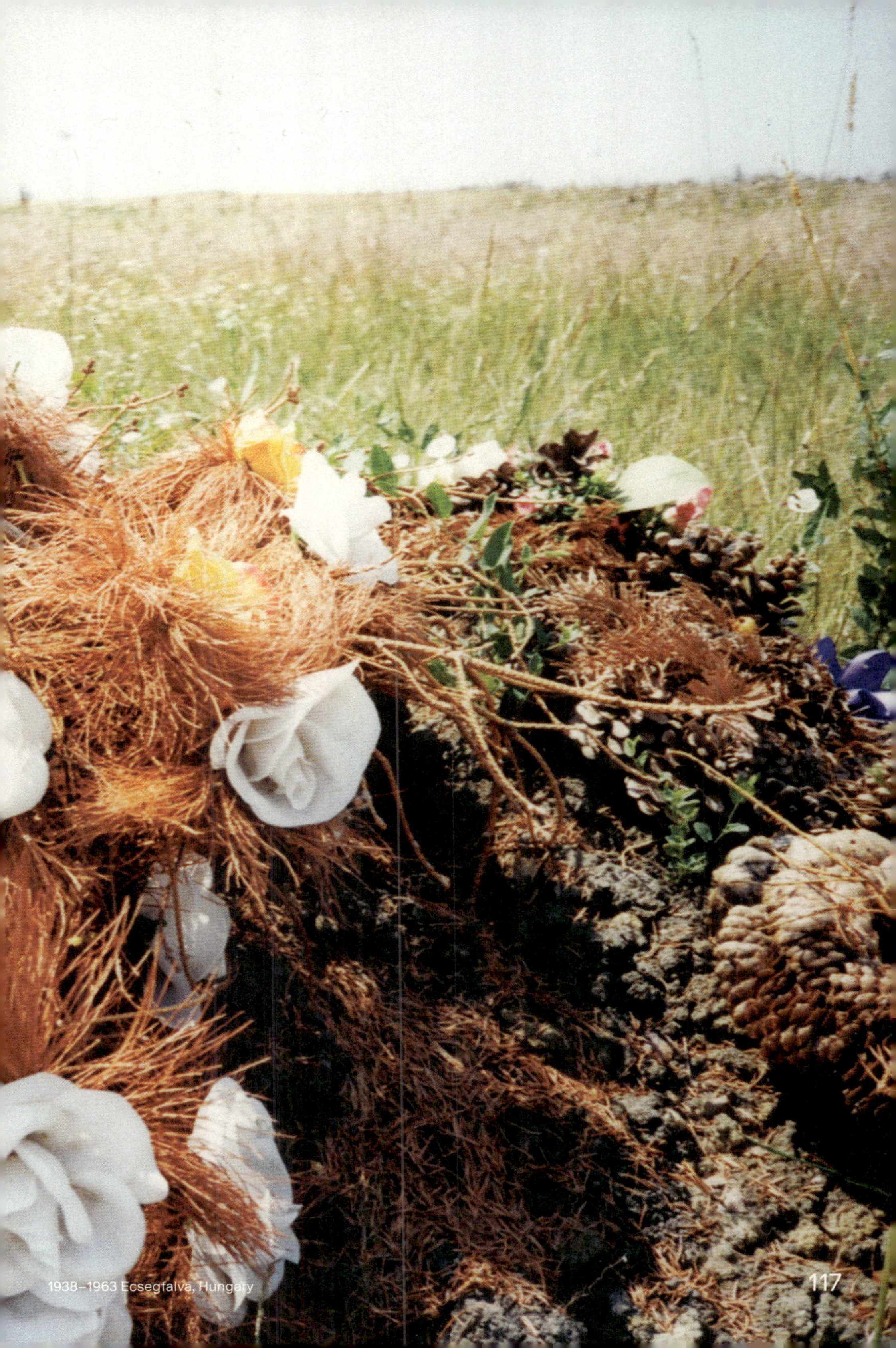

1938–1963 Ecsegfalva, Hungary

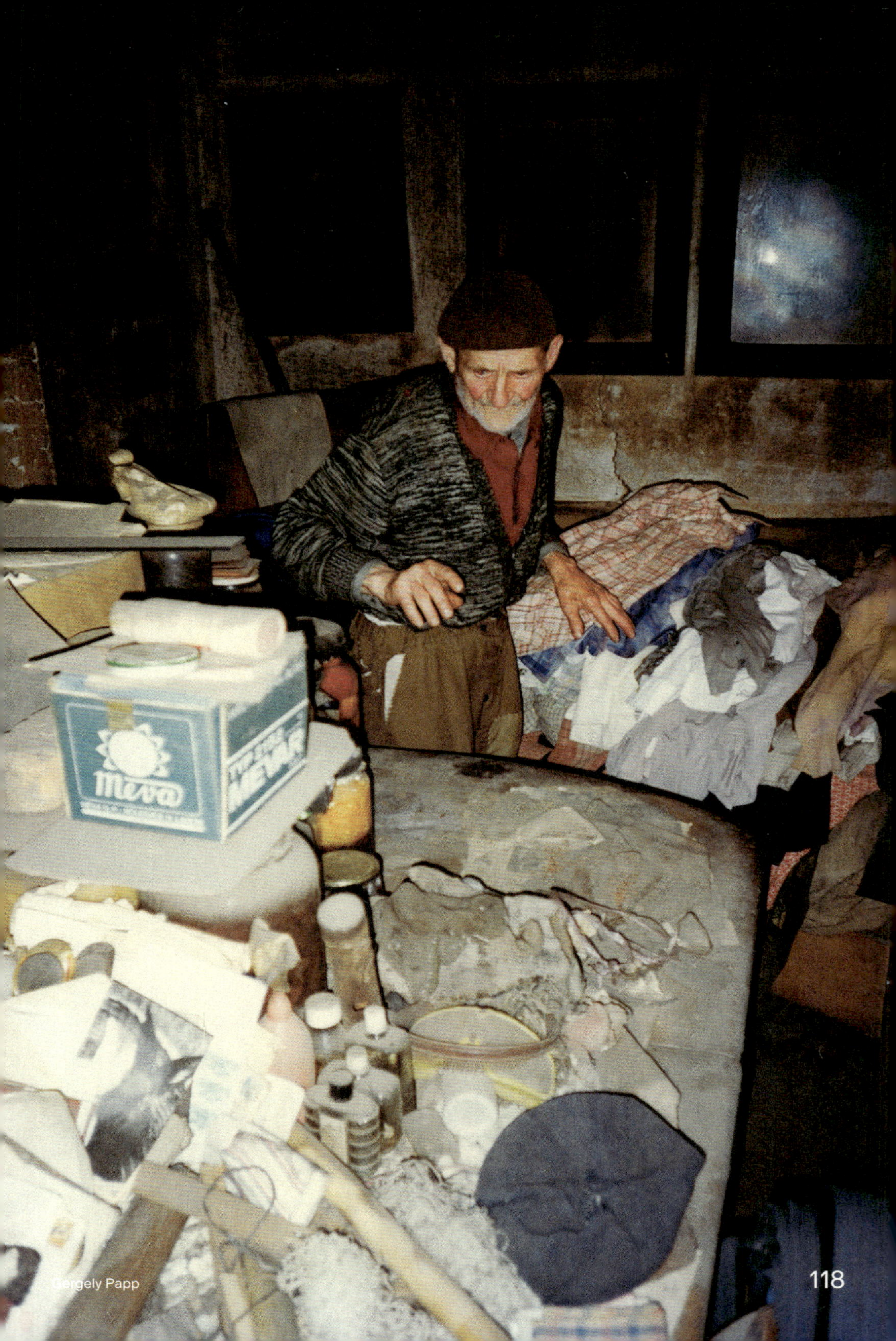

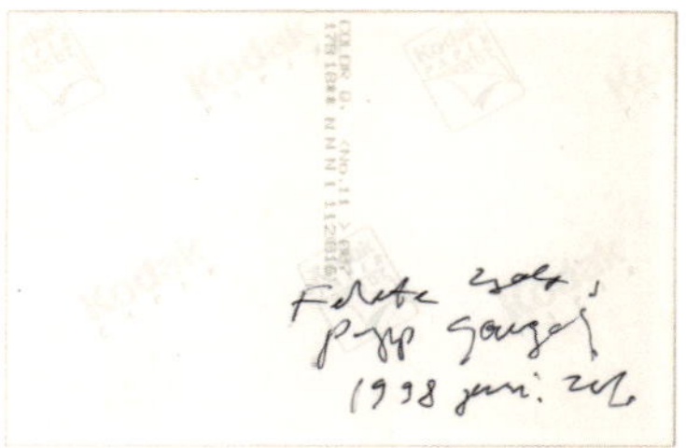

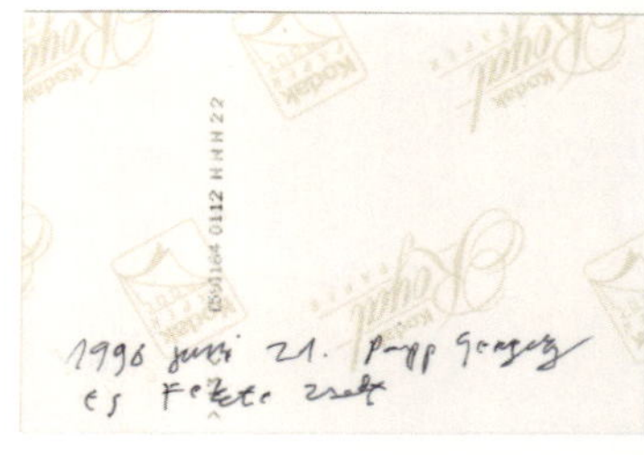

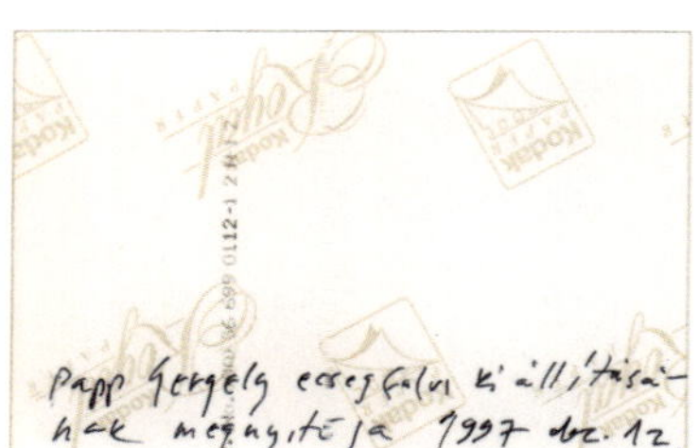

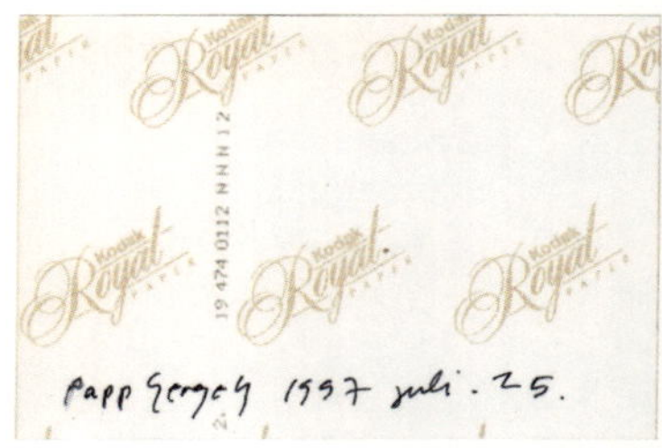

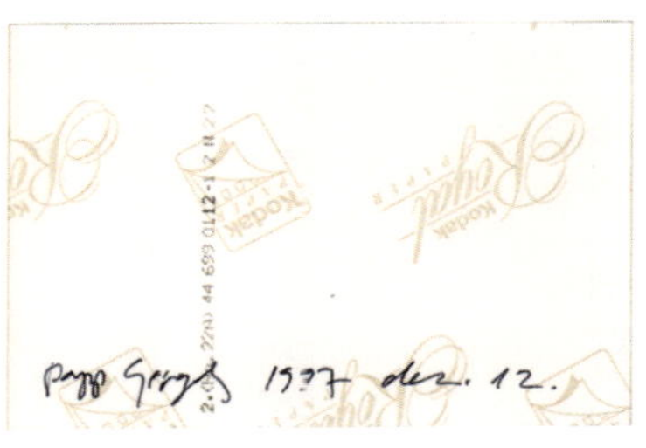

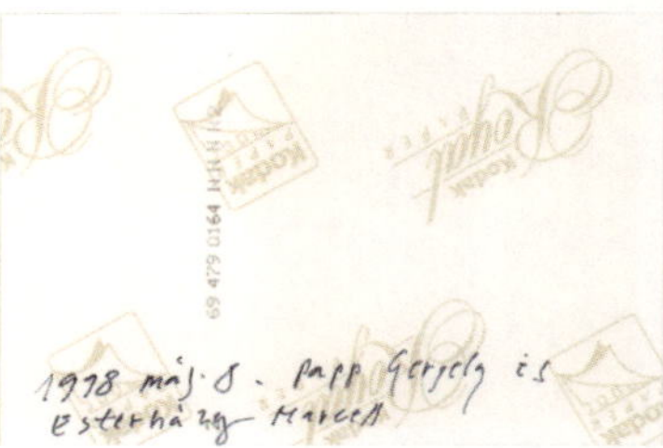

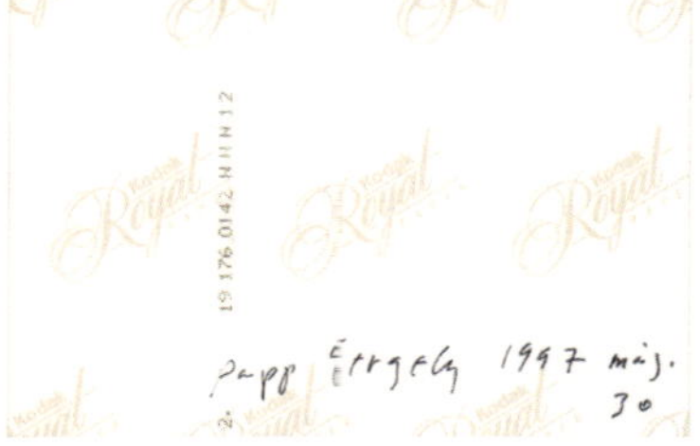

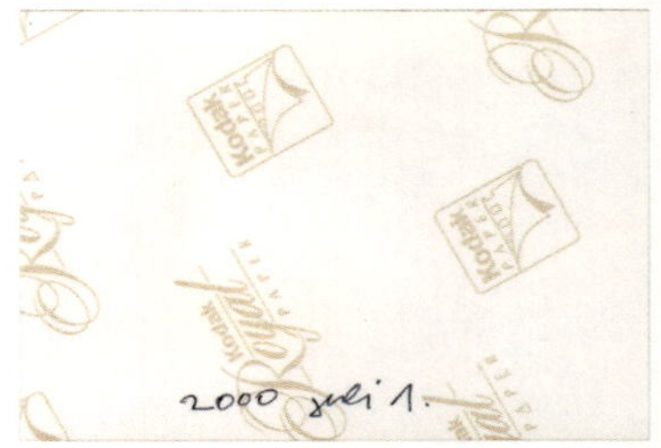

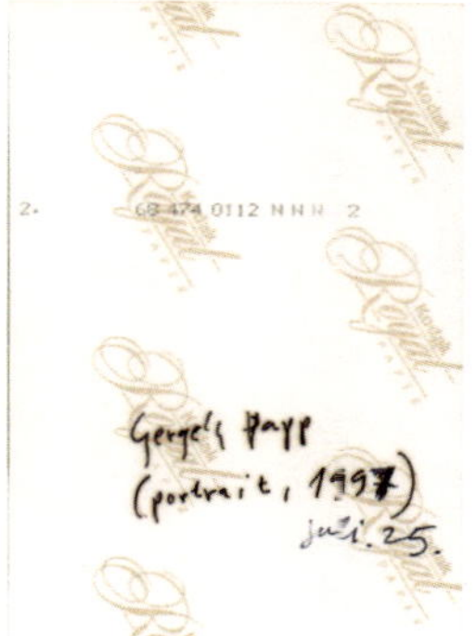

1938–1963 Ecsegfalva, Hungary

Bibliography

BOOKS
Miltényi, Tibor.
Az Esszenciális-forma [on Essential Form]. Budakeszi: Bohony Könyvkiado [Bohony Publishing House], 1999.

Miltényi, Tibor. *Isten Technikusai [God's Technicians]*. Budakeszi: Bohony Könyvkiado [Bohony Publishing House], 2006.

Miltényi, Tibor. *Papp Gergely*. Vol. 3. Szellemkép Könyvek [Ghost Books]. Budapest: Szellemkép Bt. [Ghost Bureau], 1998.

MAGAZINE ARTICLES
Miltényi, Tibor. "Eyemazing Gallery 229: Gergely Papp." *Eyemazing*, 2011, 76–89.

Miltényi, Tibor. "Gergely Papp The Photographer in Hiding." *Photographers International*, No. 55, April 2001, 8–90.

Miltényi, Tibor. "Archìv üzenet 2. (Papp Gergely Fotóiról)." *SZELLEMKÉP*, 1997, 28–46.

Miltényi, Tibor. "The Collection of Photographs by Gergely Papp (Hungary)." *Imago*, Summer 1997.

WEB ARTICLES
Miltényi, Tibor. "PAPP GERGELY ÉS AZ ESSZENCIÁLIS-FORMA." Phoo Magazine. April 11, 2016. Accessed May 08, 2018. http://phoo.hu/2016/04/11/papp-gergely-es-az-esszencialis-forma/.

EXHIBITIONS
Papp, Gergely. 7–25 April 1999. Photographs of Gergely Papp 1938–1998, Gallery Fészek, Budapest, Kertész U. 36, 1073 Hungary.

Image Index

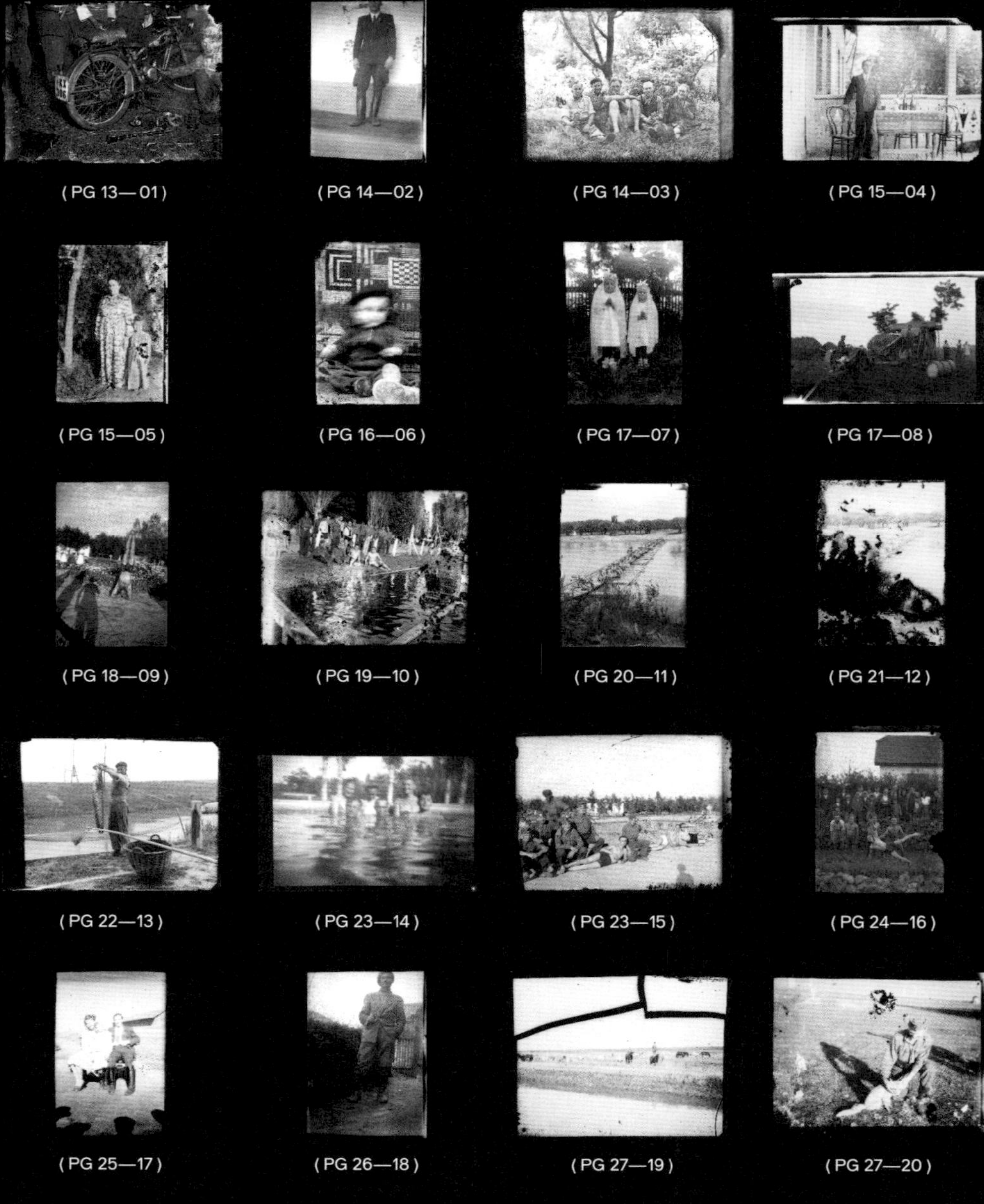

(PG 13—01) (PG 14—02) (PG 14—03) (PG 15—04)

(PG 15—05) (PG 16—06) (PG 17—07) (PG 17—08)

(PG 18—09) (PG 19—10) (PG 20—11) (PG 21—12)

(PG 22—13) (PG 23—14) (PG 23—15) (PG 24—16)

(PG 25—17) (PG 26—18) (PG 27—19) (PG 27—20)

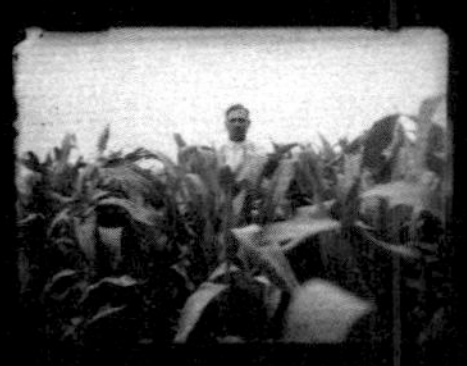

(PG 29—21)

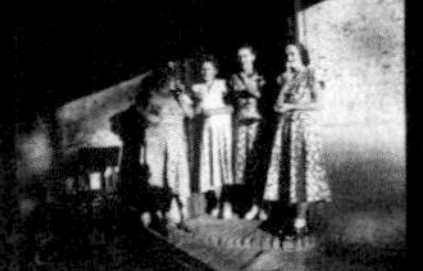

(PG 30—22)

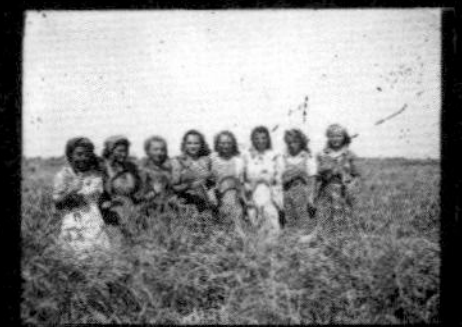
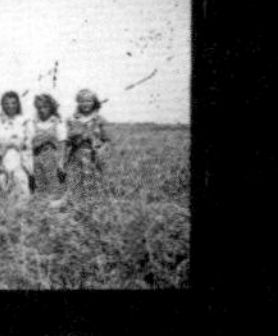

(PG 30—23)

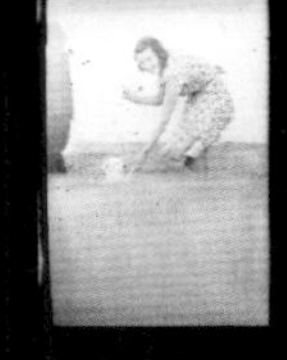

(PG 31—24)

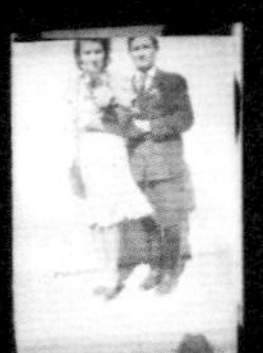

(PG 32—25)

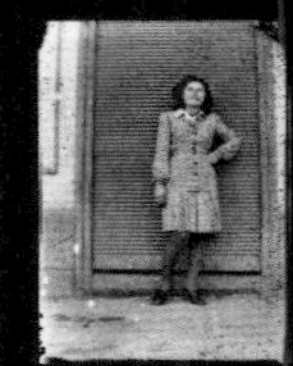

(PG 33—26)

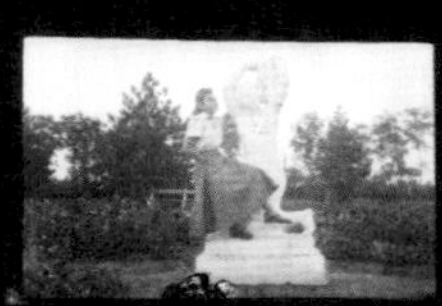

(PG 33—27)

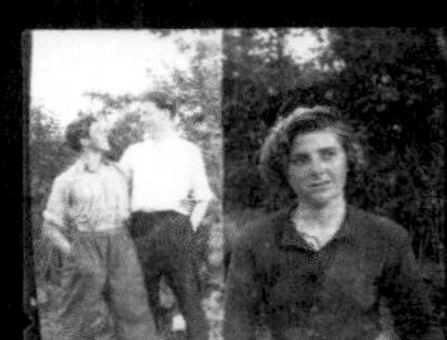

(PG 34—28)

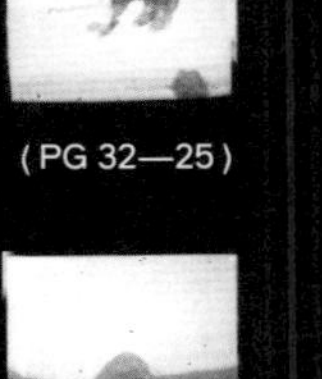

(PG 35—29)

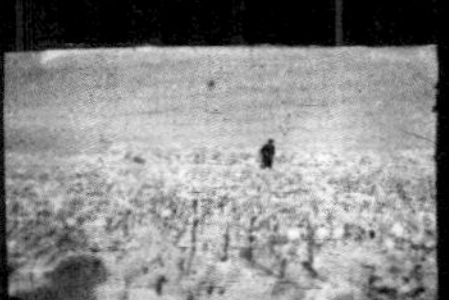

(PG 36—30)

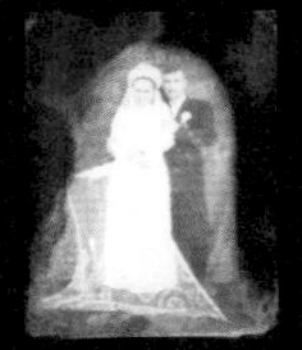

(PG 37—31)

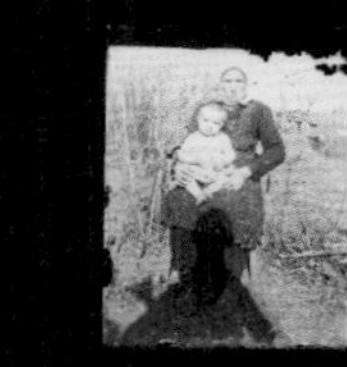

(PG 37—32)

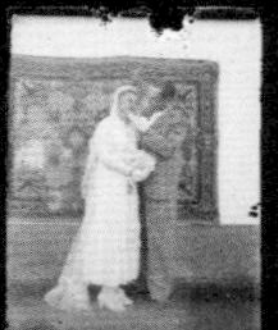

(PG 38—33)

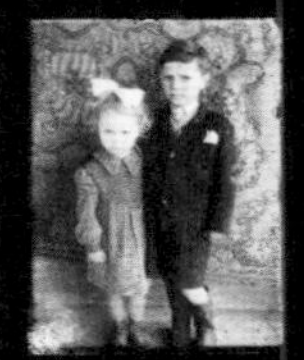

(PG 39—34)

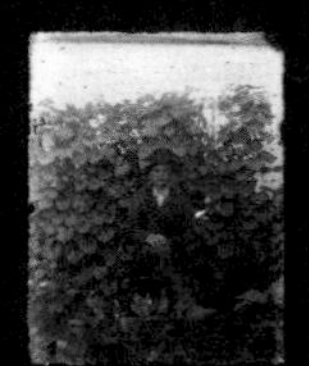

(PG 40—35)

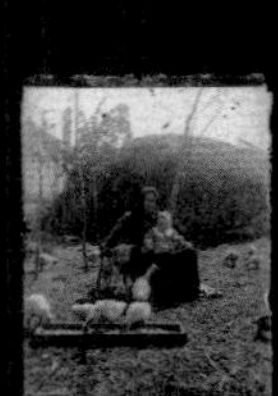

(PG 41—36)

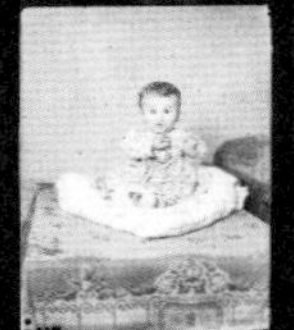

(PG 42—37)

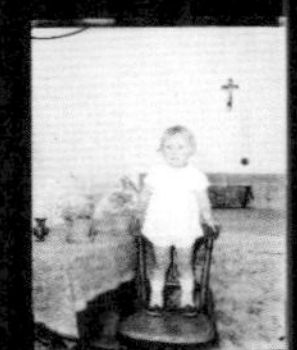

(PG 43—38)

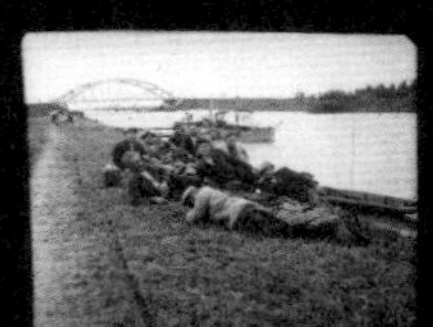

(PG 44—39)

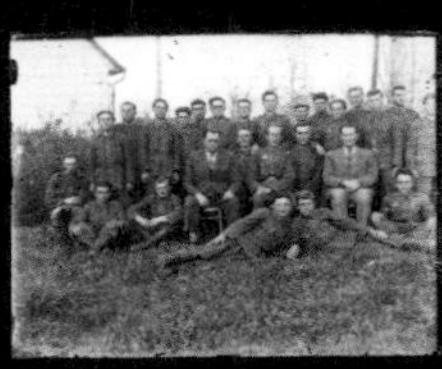

(PG 44—40)

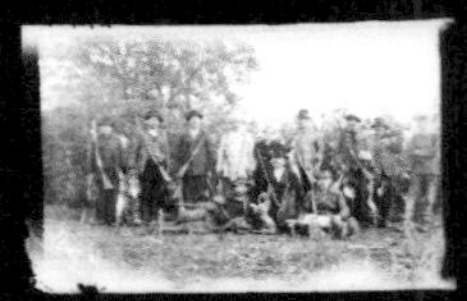

(PG 45—41)

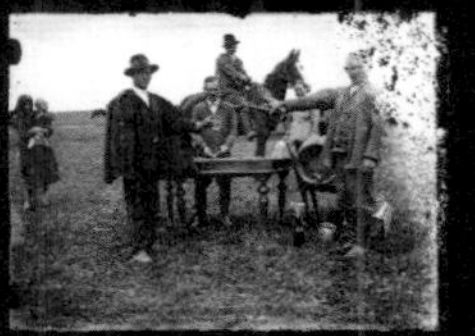

(PG 47—42)

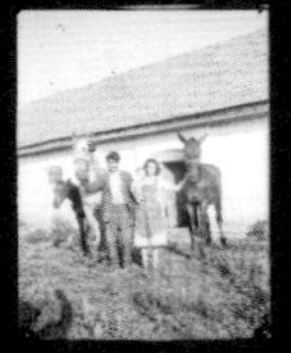

(PG 48—43)

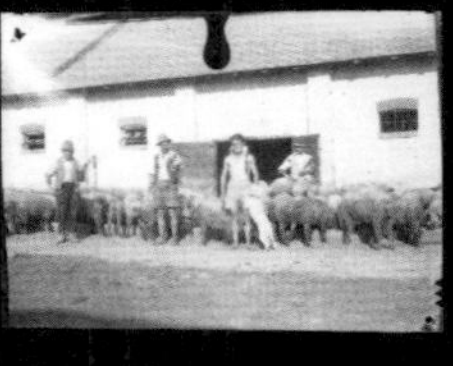

(PG 48—44)

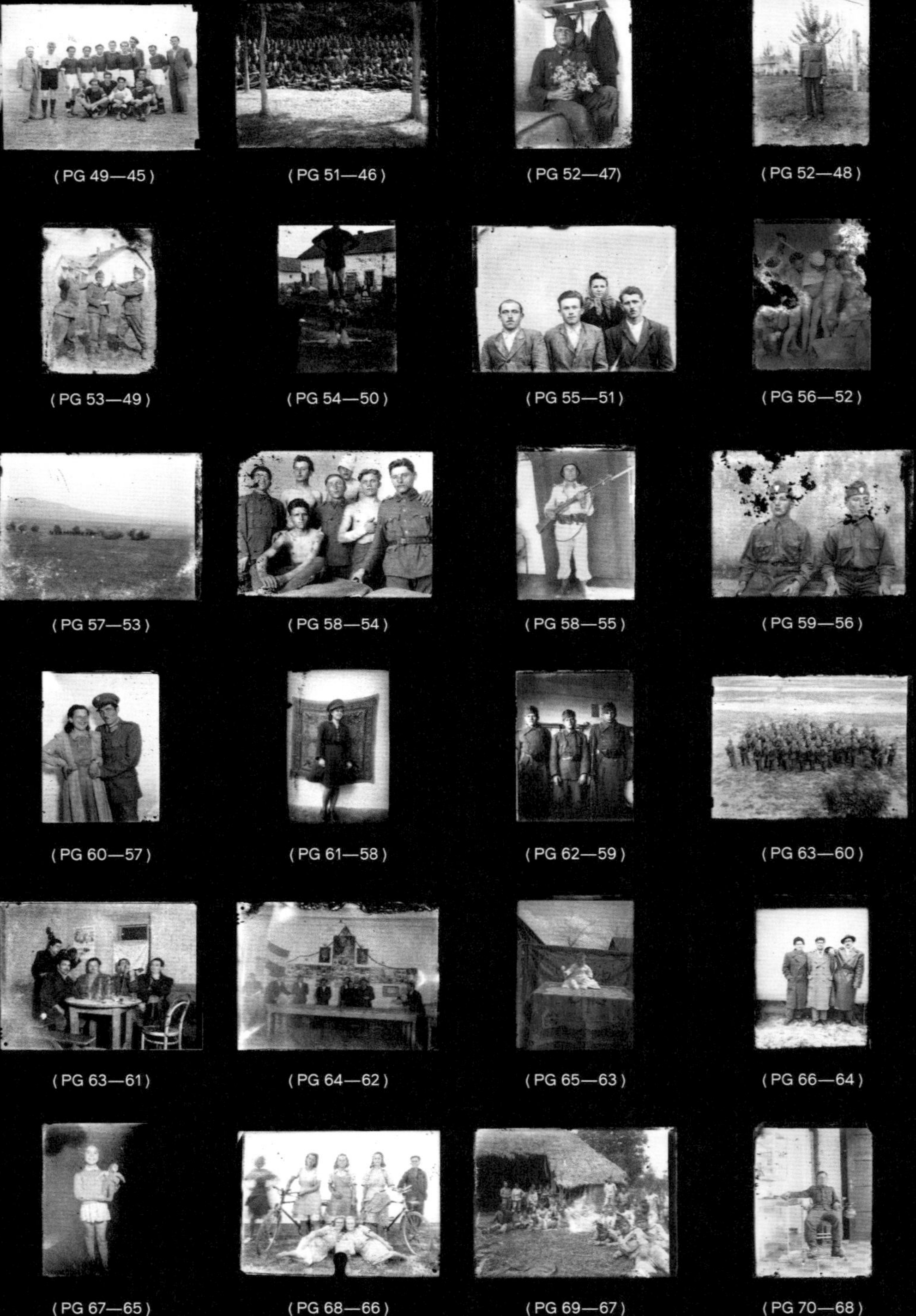

(PG 49—45) (PG 51—46) (PG 52—47) (PG 52—48)

(PG 53—49) (PG 54—50) (PG 55—51) (PG 56—52)

(PG 57—53) (PG 58—54) (PG 58—55) (PG 59—56)

(PG 60—57) (PG 61—58) (PG 62—59) (PG 63—60)

(PG 63—61) (PG 64—62) (PG 65—63) (PG 66—64)

(PG 67—65) (PG 68—66) (PG 69—67) (PG 70—68)

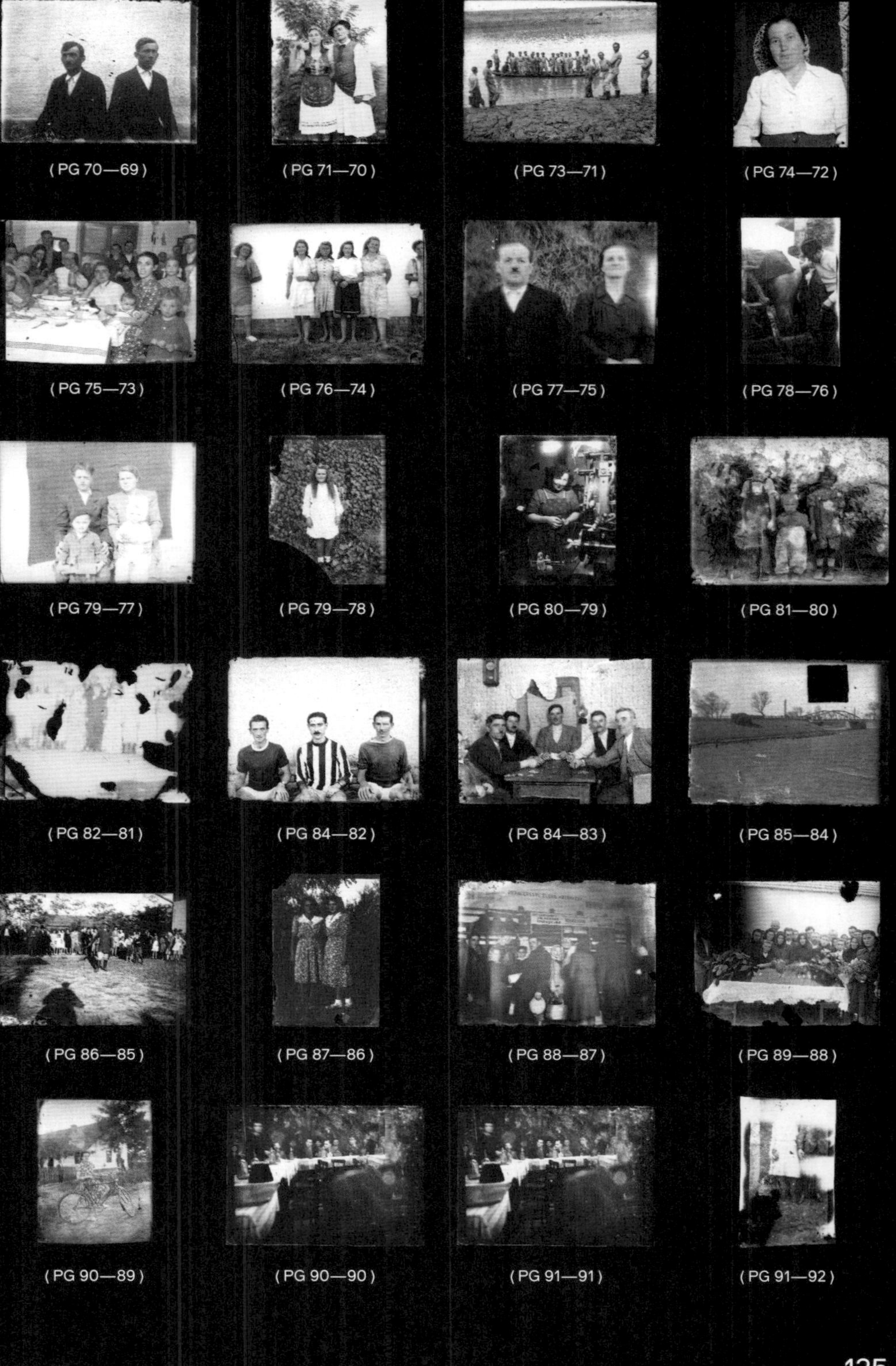

(PG 70—69) (PG 71—70) (PG 73—71) (PG 74—72)

(PG 75—73) (PG 76—74) (PG 77—75) (PG 78—76)

(PG 79—77) (PG 79—78) (PG 80—79) (PG 81—80)

(PG 82—81) (PG 84—82) (PG 84—83) (PG 85—84)

(PG 86—85) (PG 87—86) (PG 88—87) (PG 89—88)

(PG 90—89) (PG 90—90) (PG 91—91) (PG 91—92)

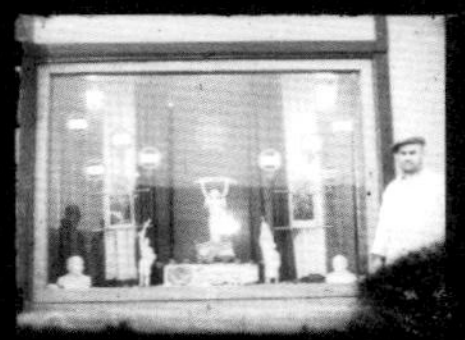
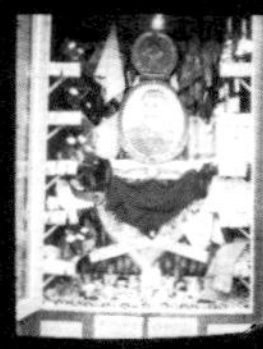
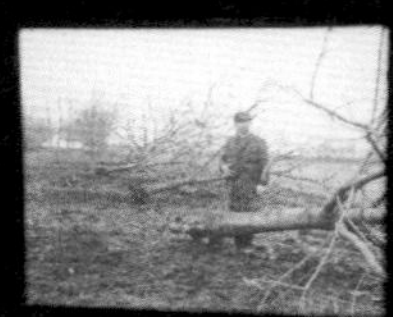

(PG 93—93)   (PG 94—94)   (PG 95—95)